2

AFRICAN POLITICAL, ECONOMIC, AND SECURITY ISSUES

AFRICAN GROWTH AND OPPORTUNITY ACT

SELECTED ANALYSES

African Political, Economic, and Security Issues

Additional books in this series can be found on Nova's website under the Series tab.

Additional e-books in this series can be found on Nova's website under the e-book tab.

AFRICAN POLITICAL, ECONOMIC, AND SECURITY ISSUES

AFRICAN GROWTH AND OPPORTUNITY ACT

SELECTED ANALYSES

HELLEN EDWARDS
EDITOR

NOVINKA

New York

Library of Congress Cataloging-in-Publication Data

ISBN: 978-1-63482-981-6

Published by Nova Science Publishers, Inc. † New York

CONTENTS

PREFACE

Signed in 2000, the African Growth and Opportunity Act (AGOA) is a trade preference program that seeks to promote economic development in 49 sub-Saharan African countries by allowing eligible countries to export qualifying goods to the United States without import duties. The act requires the U.S. government to conduct an annual eligibility review to assess each country's progress on economic, political, and development reform objectives in order to be eligible for AGOA benefits. AGOA also requires an annual forum to foster closer economic ties between the United States and sub-Saharan African countries. This book examines U.S. government TCB assistance in support of AGOA; the extent to which U.S. Agency for International Development (USAID) has made efforts to develop strategic approaches to AGOA utilization; how the AGOA eligibility review process has considered economic, political, and development reform objectives described in the act; and how sub-Saharan African countries have fared in certain economic development outcomes since the enactment of AGOA.

In: African Growth and Opportunity Act
Editor: Hellen Edwards
ISBN: 978-1-63482-981-6

Chapter 1

AFRICAN GROWTH AND OPPORTUNITY ACT: USAID COULD ENHANCE UTILIZATION BY WORKING WITH MORE COUNTRIES TO DEVELOP EXPORT STRATEGIES*

United States Government Accountability Office

ABBREVIATION

AGOA	African Growth and Opportunity Act
FTA	free trade agreement
GSP	Generalized System of Preferences
IPR	intellectual property rights
MCC	Millennium Challenge Corporation
RTA	regional trade agreement
SPS	sanitary and phyto-sanitary
TBT	technical barriers to trade
TCB	trade capacity building
USAID	U.S. Agency for International Development
USITC	U.S. International Trade Commission
USTDA	U.S. Trade and Development Agency

* This is an edited, reformatted and augmented version of The United States Government Accountability Office publication, GAO-15-218, dated January 2015.

USTR	Office of the U.S. Trade Representative
WTO	World Trade Organization

Why GAO Did This Study

Signed in 2000, AGOA directs the President to provide TCB assistance to sub-Saharan African governments and firms to promote exports and develop infrastructure, among other things. AGOA provides duty-free access on qualifying U.S. imports from eligible sub-Saharan African countries, a total of 41 countries as of December 1, 2014. From 2001 through 2013, U.S. agencies funded about $5 billion in TCB assistance to AGOA countries. GAO was asked to review various issues related to the ability of AGOA countries to utilize AGOA prior to its expiration on September 30, 2015.

In this report, GAO examines (1) U.S. government TCB assistance in support of AGOA, and (2) the extent to which USAID has made efforts to develop strategic approaches to AGOA utilization. GAO focused on MCC and USAID because these two agencies accounted for nearly 90 percent of funding for TCB activities in AGOA countries from 2001 through 2013. GAO analyzed data on U.S. TCB assistance to AGOA countries in this period, reviewed agencies' funding and program documents, conducted interviews with officials who implement U.S. TCB assistance, and met with U.S. and foreign government officials and private sector representatives in Ethiopia and Ghana.

What GAO Recommends

GAO recommends that the Administrator of USAID work with more host governments to develop strategic approaches to promoting exports under AGOA. USAID agreed with the recommendation.

What GAO Found

Among U.S. agencies, the Millennium Challenge Corporation (MCC) and the U.S. Agency for International Development (USAID) have funded the majority of trade capacity building (TCB) assistance in support of the African

Growth and Opportunity Act (AGOA) (see figure). MCC obligated nearly $3 billion in funding for TCB activities in 15 of the 41 countries eligible for AGOA (AGOA countries), with the majority of funds provided for trade-related infrastructure projects. For example, MCC obligated $176 million for a roads project in Mozambique that aimed to improve the transportation network, including access to markets and reduction of transport costs. USAID obligated approximately $1.6 billion in funding for TCB activities in 39 of the 41 AGOA countries, with the majority of funds provided for trade-related agriculture and infrastructure, and trade facilitation. For example, USAID funded activities to help exporters in East Africa build business linkages with U.S. markets through trade shows.

U.S. Trade Capacity Building (TCB) Funding Obligated for African Growth and Opportunity Act Countries by Category, 2001-2013

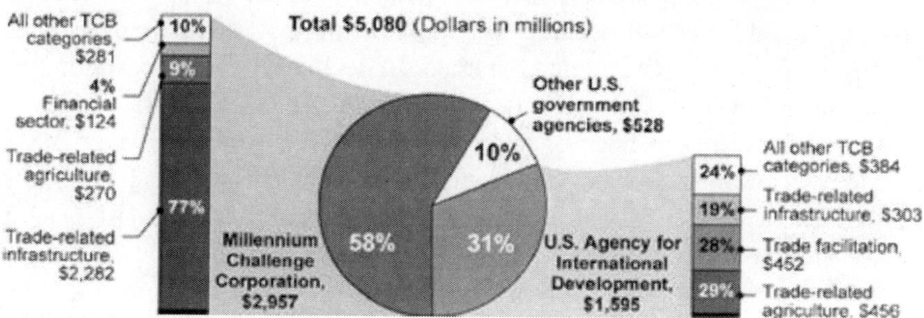

Source: GAO analysis of USAID data. | GAO-15-218.

Note: Funding amounts or percentages may not sum to totals because of rounding.

USAID has worked with some host governments to develop strategic approaches to AGOA utilization; however, most host governments have not established such approaches. USAID-funded regional trade hubs in sub-Saharan Africa have supported AGOA utilization by, among other things, collaborating with some host governments to develop AGOA-specific or broader national export strategies. Trade hub evaluations and statements from host government officials show that identifying strategic needs and priorities through strategic approaches can bolster AGOA utilization and help assess challenges to expanding exports. In strategy documents, host governments may identify high-priority trade and investment sectors, constraints related to AGOA utilization, and specific steps to increase exports under AGOA. Lack of a strategic approach has been identified as a significant reason for gaps in AGOA utilization. As of December 2014, 14 of the 41 AGOA countries had strategies reflecting AGOA priorities. According to USAID officials, host governments must initiate the process of developing a strategy, and a lack of political will may pose challenges to such efforts.

January 22, 2015

Congressional Requesters

The African Growth and Opportunity Act (AGOA), signed into law in 2000,[1] is a U.S. trade preference program that allows eligible sub-Saharan African countries to export qualifying goods to the United States without import duties.[2] AGOA is intended to promote free markets, stimulate economic development in sub-Saharan Africa through export-led growth, and facilitate sub-Saharan Africa's integration into the global economy. U.S. imports from countries eligible for AGOA, which we generally refer to as AGOA countries, have increased since 2001, although these countries' share of overall U.S. imports have remained small and experienced declines in recent years. In 2013, 2 percent of overall U.S. imports came from AGOA countries.[3] To help countries take full advantage of increased trading opportunities under AGOA, U.S. agencies have provided various forms of technical assistance commonly referred to as trade capacity building (TCB) support.[4] This assistance may include support for addressing the regulatory environment for business, trade, and investment; improving customs procedures; and developing infrastructure, such as ports and roads. U.S. and African officials have recognized the need for continued trade capacity building to help sub-Saharan African countries make better use of AGOA. Most recently, in conjunction with the U.S.-Africa Leaders Summit, held in Washington, D.C., in August 2014, President Obama stated that in order for countries to be able to utilize AGOA to its fullest, AGOA must be linked to a comprehensive, coordinated trade and investment capacity-building approach.[5] The President also called for a comprehensive U.S. approach to expanding sub-Saharan Africa's capacity for trade and investment.

As Congress deliberates reauthorization of AGOA, which is set to expire on September 30, 2015, policymakers have expressed interest in countries' ability to utilize AGOA and U.S. TCB assistance in support of AGOA. In this report, we focus on the Millennium Challenge Corporation (MCC) and the U.S. Agency for International Development (USAID), the U.S. agencies providing the most funding for TCB activities in AGOA countries. MCC reports that it conducts TCB-related activities in AGOA countries that support its agency goals but does not have a specific TCB mission. In addition to providing funding for TCB assistance to AGOA countries, USAID includes assistance for increasing exports through TCB among its development objectives, and also has a worldwide strategy focused entirely on TCB. In this strategy, USAID notes that its TCB projects, among other things, will help developing countries take advantage of the opportunities created by trade and trade preference programs such as AGOA.[6]

Congressional requesters asked us to examine a number of issues relating to AGOA countries' trade expansion and economic development, and factors affecting their trade with the United States and other countries.[7] In this report, the second in a series responding to the request, we examine (1) U.S. government TCB assistance in support of AGOA, and (2) the extent to which USAID has made efforts to develop strategic approaches to AGOA utilization.[8]

To address both objectives, we interviewed officials from the Departments of Commerce, State, and the Treasury; MCC; and USAID; but focused on MCC and USAID for the purposes of this report. We also interviewed officials from the Office of the U.S. Trade Representative (USTR) and the U.S. International Trade Commission (USITC), agencies that do not provide funding for U.S. TCB assistance but provided additional contextual information on AGOA and TCB. We reviewed documents related to the three USAID-funded trade hubs and other U.S. TCB assistance, and examples of AGOA-specific and national export strategies. We also conducted fieldwork in Ethiopia and Ghana, where we interviewed U.S. agency and host government officials, representatives from the private sector, and U.S.-funded contractors implementing TCB activities. We selected these two countries because they represented a cross section of U.S. TCB assistance and are in different regions within sub-Saharan Africa, but our findings from these countries are not generalizable to the universe of all U.S. TCB activities in AGOA countries. To examine U.S. government TCB assistance in support of AGOA, we reviewed documents from relevant U.S. agencies, including program descriptions and evaluations, and analyzed data USAID provided on U.S. TCB obligations for all AGOA countries from fiscal years 2001 through 2013. In assessing the data, we interviewed key USAID officials and the contractor responsible for administering the database, reviewed supporting documentation, and determined that the data were sufficiently reliable for our purposes. To examine the extent to which USAID has made efforts to develop strategic approaches to AGOA utilization, we reviewed documents from relevant U.S. agencies, including program descriptions and evaluations, and information on

AGOA-specific and national export strategies from U.S. agencies and host governments.[9] Appendix I provides a detailed discussion of our objectives, scope, and methodology.

We conducted this performance audit from March 2014 to January 2015 in accordance with generally accepted government auditing standards. Those standards require that we plan and perform the audit to obtain sufficient, appropriate evidence to provide a reasonable basis for our findings and conclusions based on our audit objectives. We believe that the evidence obtained provides a reasonable basis for our findings and conclusions based on our audit objectives.

BACKGROUND

African Growth and Opportunity Act

AGOA is a trade preference program that provides eligible sub-Saharan African countries duty-free access to U.S. markets for more than 6,000 dutiable items in the U.S. import tariff schedules.[10] AGOA also includes goals related to U.S. government technical assistance in sub-Saharan Africa. Countries must meet certain eligibility criteria to take advantage of AGOA preferences,[11] and the program had 41 such eligible countries as of December 1, 2014.[12]

AGOA legislation directs the President to target technical assistance to serve specific TCB-related goals that promote economic reform and development, and to develop and implement certain policies aimed at encouraging investment in sub-Saharan Africa.[13] With regard to technical assistance, AGOA directs the President to focus such assistance on the following goals:

1. Develop relationships between U.S. and sub-Saharan African firms through business associations and networks.
2. Provide assistance to the governments of sub-Saharan African countries aimed at
   - liberalizing trade and promoting exports,
   - bringing legal regimes into compliance with the standards of the World Trade Organization,
   - making financial and fiscal reforms, and

- promoting greater agribusiness linkages.

3. Address critical agriculture policy issues such as market liberalization, agriculture export development, and agribusiness investment in processing and transporting agriculture commodities.
4. Increase the number of reverse trade missions to growth-oriented countries in sub-Saharan Africa.[14]
5. Increase trade in services.[15]
6. Encourage greater sub-Saharan African participation in future negotiations in the World Trade Organization (WTO) on services and making further commitments to encourage the removal of tariff and nontariff barriers.

Trade-Related Challenges in Sub-Saharan Africa

According to research literature, AGOA countries face various challenges that affect opportunities to facilitate trade. For example, firms in AGOA countries may lack the marketing expertise, market information, and business contacts to effectively export to the U.S. market. Literature also notes challenges sub-Saharan African countries face in certain manufacturing sectors, including problems with cost and quality of inputs, access to finance, trade logistics such as the high cost of transporting goods, and inadequate workforce skills. The International Finance Corporation, a member of the World Bank Group, has reported that less than a quarter of adults in sub-Saharan Africa have access to formal financial services, and lack of access to finance is a constraint to economic growth overall, and the growth of small and medium-sized enterprises in the region.[16] Another study found that AGOA apparel production is concentrated in low-skill tasks with little knowledge transfer to local workers, and that the global competitiveness of AGOA exporters still depends on the preferences they receive under AGOA.[17] Many AGOA countries lack the capacity to produce and export goods in the necessary quantity and at the quality U.S. markets require. This same challenge may also affect potential investors' decisions about engaging in Africa.

Literature on AGOA and TCB has also shown that poor infrastructure conditions in sub-Saharan Africa remain a key challenge that undermines export competitiveness. In 2014, USITC reported that weak transportation infrastructure, including poor rural roads, inefficient port facilities, and burdensome customs procedures are among the impediments to export growth and competitiveness for sub-Saharan Africa. [18] The report noted that a number of factors directly affect the cost and timeliness of delivery of goods to the U.S. market, including distance to market, perishability of products, freight rates, and reliability of trade linkages.

Trade Capacity Building Assistance

Since at least 2001, the United States has provided TCB assistance to developing countries to help them participate in and benefit from global trade. U.S agencies generally define TCB broadly to include all types of development assistance that enhance a country's ability to secure benefits from international trade. Among other things, such assistance can address (1) the regulatory environment for business, trade, and investment; (2) constraints such as low capacity for production and entrepreneurship; and (3) inadequate physical infrastructure, such as poor transport and storage facilities. USAID collects data to identify and quantify the U.S. government's TCB activities in developing countries through an annual survey of U.S. agencies and maintains the survey results in the U.S. government's publicly available online TCB database.[19] This database of TCB funding defines 14 categories of TCB assistance provided by the U.S. government (see app. II for a detailed list of TCB category definitions and examples of related activities). The majority of U.S. TCB funding for AGOA countries from 2001 through 2013 was provided for three categories of activities: trade-related infrastructure, trade-related agriculture, and trade facilitation (see fig. 1).

Funding by Key U.S. Agencies for TCB Assistance for AGOA Countries

Total U.S. government funding for TCB assistance for AGOA countries from 2001 to 2013 was approximately $5 billion. In that time period, U.S. government TCB assistance for AGOA countries peaked in 2008 and declined sharply in 2012 (see fig. 2).

The U.S. government provided funding for TCB assistance from 2001 through 2013 for all 41 AGOA countries. Sixty-eight percent of all U.S. government TCB funding obligated for AGOA countries from 2001 through 2013 was for 10 of these countries (see table 1).

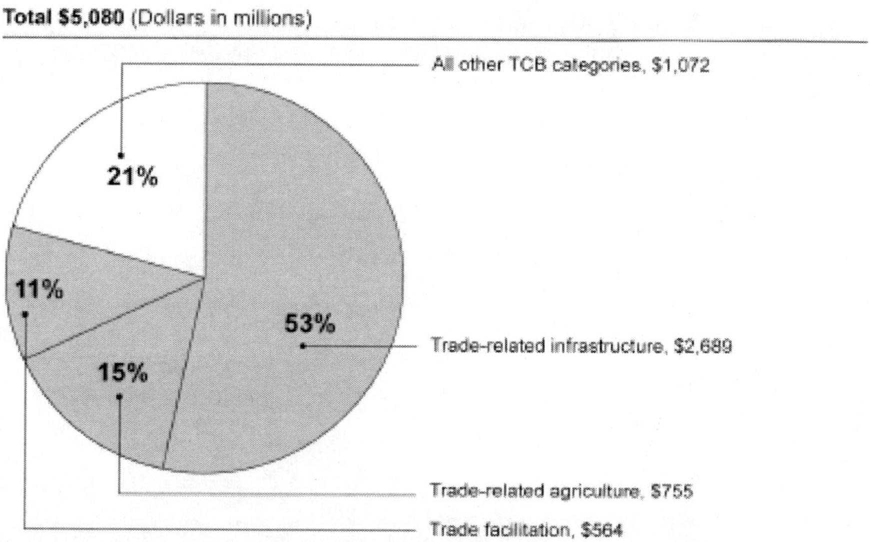

Source: GAO analysis of USAID data. | GAO -15-218.

Note: This figure includes U.S. government TCB funding provided for individual AGOA countries as well as funding that U.S. agencies account for under four regional groupings: sub-Saharan Africa, East and Central Africa, Western Africa, and Southern Africa.

Figure 1. U.S. Trade Capacity Building (TCB) Funding Obligated for African Growth and Opportunity Act (AGOA) Countries by Category, 2001-2013.

Although the President affirmed the U.S. government's commitment to providing TCB assistance for AGOA countries in August 2014, no single agency is responsible. According to our analysis of the U.S. government's TCB database, MCC and USAID are the agencies that reported providing the most funding for AGOA countries, and accounted for 90 percent of all TCB assistance to these countries from 2001 through 2013 (see fig. 3). While USAID funds activities that have clear and direct links to TCB, MCC funds activities that may be more indirectly related to international trade. MCC conducts TCB-related activities that support its broader strategic and agency goals.20 In contrast, one of USAID's core development objectives is to promote sustainable, broad-based economic growth by helping developing countries increase their exports through trade capacity building. USAID aims to achieve its TCB goal by supporting participation in trade negotiations, implementation of trade agreements, and economic responsiveness to trade opportunities. USAID also collects data to identify and quantify the U.S.

government's TCB activities through an annual survey of U.S. agencies and maintains the survey results in the U.S. government's publicly available online TCB database.[21]

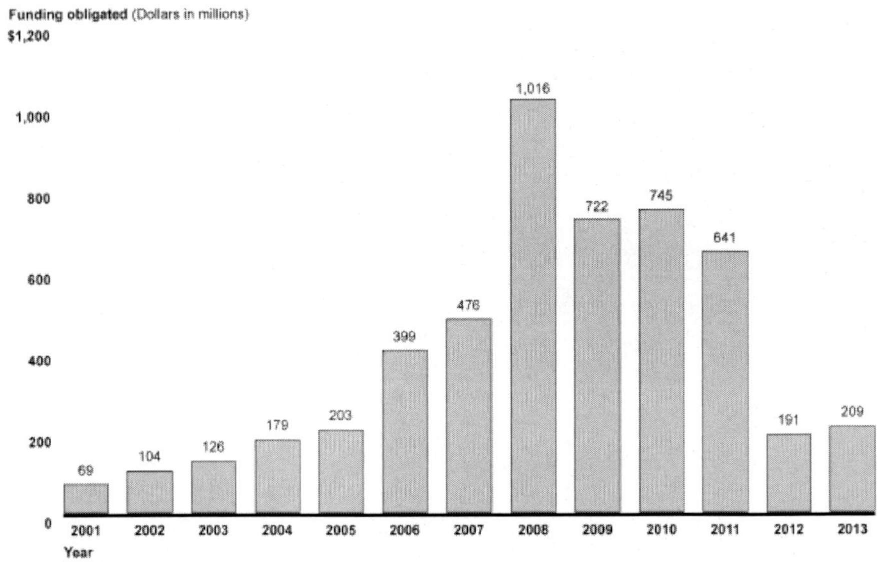

Source: GAO analysis of USAID data. | GAO -15-218.

Notes: This figure includes U.S. government TCB funding provided for individual AGOA countries as well as funding that U.S. agencies account for under four regional groupings: sub-Saharan Africa, East and Central Africa, Western Africa, and Southern Africa.

Funding in any given year may appear distorted because the Millennium Challenge Corporation (MCC) obligates its funding in the year in which its compacts enter into force. As a result, MCC funding is concentrated in certain years in the figure above, even though the distribution of funds occurred over several years.

MCC was created in 2004 and signed the first compact agreements in 2005.

Figure 2. U.S. Government Trade Capacity Building (TCB) Funding Obligated for African Growth and Opportunity Act (AGOA) Countries by Year, 2001-2013.

Table 1. U.S. Government Trade Capacity Building (TCB) Funding Obligated for African Growth and Opportunity Act (AGOA) Countries by Country, 2001-2013

Dollars in millions

AGOA country	Total TCB funding	Percentage of total
Tanzania	676	13
Senegal	517	10
Burkina Faso	408	8
Malawi	403	8
Ghana	373	7
Mozambique	292	6
Ethiopia	212	4
Benin	192	4
South Sudan	189	4
Mali	189	4
All other AGOA countriesa	1,629	32
Total	5,080	100

Source: GAO analysis of USAID data. | GAO-15-218.

[a]This table includes U.S. government TCB funding provided for individual AGOA countries as well as funding that U.S. agencies account for under four regional groupings: sub-Saharan Africa, East and Central Africa, Western Africa, and Southern Africa.

MCC's and USAID's TCB Assistance in Support of AGOA Has Primarily Focused on Barriers to Trade-Related Infrastructure and Agriculture, and Trade Facilitation

MCC Has Taken Steps to Support AGOA through TCB Assistance That Is Generally Focused on Trade-Related Infrastructure Needs, but Broader Infrastructure Challenges Remain

MCC's TCB-related activities in sub-Saharan Africa are supportive of AGOA. MCC identifies a relationship between AGOA and the agency's role in improving economic growth, including through its trade-related infrastructure activities in selected sub-Saharan African countries.

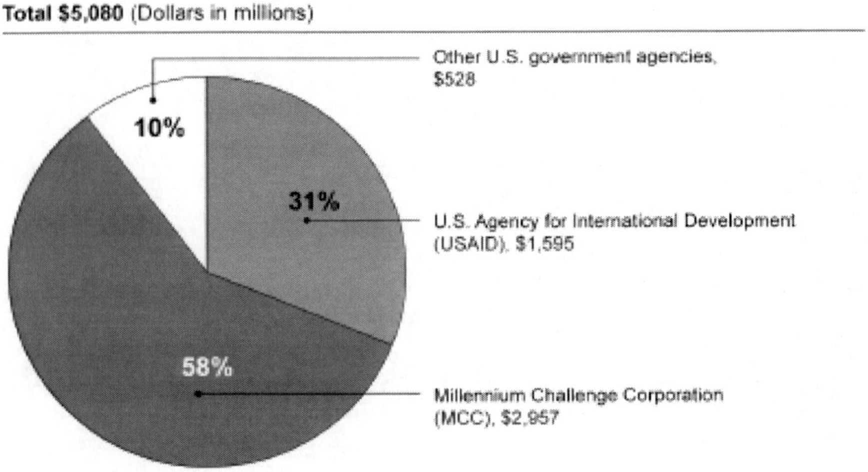

Source: GAO analysis of USAID data. | GAO -15-218.

Notes: Funding amounts or percentages may not sum to totals because of rounding. This figure includes U.S. government TCB funding provided for individual AGOA countries as well as funding that U.S. agencies account for under four regional groupings: sub-Saharan Africa, East and Central Africa, Western Africa, and Southern Africa.

MCC was created in 2004 and signed the first compact agreements in 2005.

Figure 3. U.S. Government Trade Capacity Building (TCB) Funding Obligated for African Growth and Opportunity Act (AGOA) Countries by Funding Agency, 2001-2013.

According to agency officials, MCC's focus on economic growth and encouraging private sector investment is in line with the goals of AGOA. Furthermore, agency officials said that MCC infrastructure-related investments have included a number of projects that support global trade in sub-Saharan Africa. From 2005 through 2013, MCC funded TCB activities in 15 of the 41 AGOA countries (see table 2).

Table 2. Millennium Challenge Corporation (MCC) Trade Capacity Building (TCB) Funding Obligated for African Growth and Opportunity Act (AGOA) Countries by Country, 2001-2013

Dollars in millions

AGOA country	*Total TCB funding*	*Percentage of total*
Tanzania	579	20
Senegal	494	17

AGOA country	*Total TCB funding*	*Percentage of total*
Burkina Faso	396	13
Malawi	351	12
Ghana	240	8
Mozambique	222	8
Benin	189	6
Mali	136	5
Cape Verde	105	4
Lesotho	100	3
Namibia	81	3
Madagascar	52	2
Zambia	6	<1
Liberia	4	<1
São Tomé and Príncipe	4	<1
Total	*2,957*	*100*

Source: GAO analysis of USAID data. | GAO-15-218.

Notes: Funding amounts or percentages may not sum to totals because of rounding. MCC was created in 2004 and signed the first compact agreements in 2005.

MCC's TCB funding for AGOA countries has supported a range of TCB activities, largely focused on trade-related infrastructure. MCC's TCB assistance in AGOA countries has covered 10 of the 14 TCB categories, with the majority of funding, over 75 percent, concentrated on trade-related infrastructure (see fig. 4).[22]

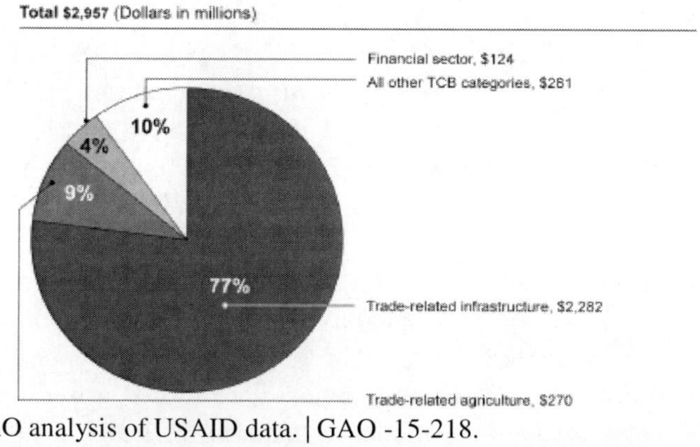

Source: GAO analysis of USAID data. | GAO -15-218.

Note: MCC was created in 2004 and signed the first compact agreements in 2005.

Figure 4. Millennium Challenge Corporation (MCC) Trade Capacity Building (TCB) Funding Obligated for African Growth and Opportunity Act Countries by Category, 2001-2013.

MCC's trade-related infrastructure projects in AGOA countries cover a range of activities including building roads, improving ports, and expanding access to electricity. For example, MCC compacts in Mozambique and Malawi include large infrastructure components, as described below:

- *Mozambique.* MCC signed a compact with Mozambique in 2007 for about $506.9 million, of which about $222 million was obligated for TCB-related activities, mostly concentrated on trade-related infrastructure. This compact included $176 million in trade-related infrastructure assistance for a roads project rehabilitating 491 kilometers of key segments of the country's transportation network The project aimed to improve access to markets, resources, and services; reduce transport costs for the private sector; and expand connectivity across the region.
- *Malawi.* MCC signed a compact with Malawi in 2011 for $350.7 million, and data show that the entire amount was obligated for trade-related infrastructure activities. Specifically, the compact is a single-sector power revitalization project that aims to increase the capacity and stability of the national electricity grid and bolster the efficiency and sustainability of hydropower generation.

Officials we spoke to in Ghana and Ethiopia, the two AGOA countries where we conducted fieldwork, highlighted a range of ongoing infrastructure improvements and challenges. Business representatives in Ghana, where MCC funded $240 million in TCB-related assistance, noted that U.S. TCB activities had helped to reduce problems with land transportation. In Ethiopia, a representative from local business noted that infrastructure challenges had been diminished through improvements in transportation, which had reduced costs for importing and exporting goods. Officials and local business representatives in both Ethiopia and Ghana also cited a range of ongoing infrastructure challenges that acted as an impediment to conducting business. For example, in Ethiopia, officials cited infrastructure issues, among others, as an impediment to conducting business in the country, and representatives of local businesses noted that further investment was needed in services such as power, roads, and telecommunications. In addition, officials in Ghana stated that port congestion caused delays, and the manufacturing sector was diminished partly because of a lack of access to reliable power.[23]

To further address infrastructure-related challenges in Africa, the U.S. government introduced two new initiatives in 2013 that will complement

AGOA. Power Africa is designed to double the number of people with access to power in sub-Saharan Africa with an initial 5-year commitment through 2018.[24] According to USTR, the initiatives of Power Africa are vital complements to AGOA. Power Africa is supported by 12 U.S. government agencies and coordinated by USAID.[25] Trade Africa is a partnership between the United States and sub-Saharan African governments to increase internal and regional trade within Africa, and expand trade and economic ties among Africa, the United States, and other global markets.[26]

USAID Has Made Efforts to Support AGOA by Funding Trade-Related Agriculture and Trade Facilitation Activities, but Challenges Remain in Facilitating Exports under AGOA

USAID's TCB funding has supported a range of TCB activities for AGOA countries, with trade-related agriculture and trade facilitation being the two largest categories. USAID has funded TCB assistance activities in 39 of 41 AGOA countries; see table 3 for AGOA countries with the highest USAID TCB funding.[27]

Table 3. USAID Trade Capacity Building (TCB) Funding Obligated for African Growth and Opportunity Act (AGOA) Countries by Country, 2001-2013

Dollars in millions

AGOA country	Total TCB funding	Percentage of total
South Sudan	189	12
Ethiopia	184	12
Ghana	86	5
Uganda	74	5
Mozambique	59	4
Rwanda	54	3
Tanzania	53	3
Mali	49	3
Liberia	45	3
Nigeria	44	3
All other AGOA countries[a]	757	47
Total	1,595	100

Source: GAO analysis of USAID data. | GAO-15-218.

Notes: Funding amounts or percentages may not sum to totals because of rounding.
[a]This table includes USAID TCB funding provided for individual AGOA countries as well as funding that USAID accounts for under four regional groupings: sub-Saharan Africa, East and Central Africa, Western Africa, and Southern Africa. According to USAID, funding for regional trade hubs is obligated to East and Central Africa, Western Africa, and Southern Africa. Sub-Saharan Africa includes TCB assistance that benefits multiple countries across different regions.

USAID's TCB assistance activities in AGOA countries covers all 14 TCB categories, with the majority of funding, over 75 percent, concentrated on trade-related agriculture, trade facilitation, and trade-related infrastructure (see fig. 5).

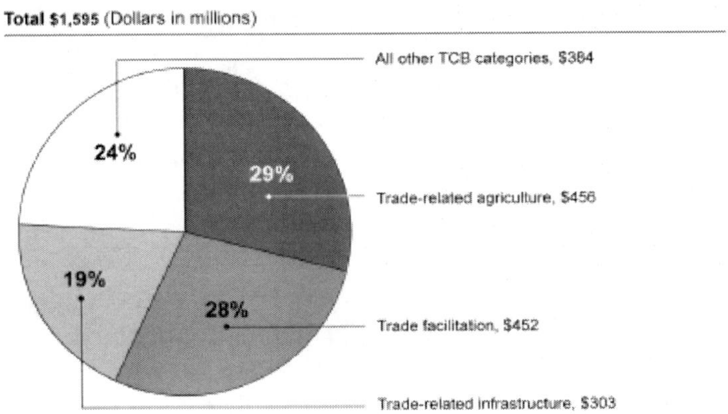

Source: GAO analysis of USAID data. | GAO-15-218.
Note: This figure includes USAID TCB funding provided for individual AGOA countries as well as funding that USAID accounts for under four regional groupings: sub-Saharan Africa, East and Central Africa, Western Africa, and Southern Africa. According to USAID, funding for regional trade hubs is obligated to East and Central Africa, Western Africa, and Southern Africa. Sub-Saharan Africa includes TCB assistance that benefits multiple countries across different regions.

Figure 5. USAID Trade Capacity Building (TCB) Funding Obligated for African Growth and Opportunity Act (AGOA) Countries by Category, 2001-2013.

From 2002 to 2004, USAID established three regional trade hubs in sub-Saharan Africa that serve as primary implementers of U.S. TCB assistance for sub-Saharan African countries (see fig. 6).[28] These USAIDfunded trade hubs are staffed with regional advisers who provide a range of services to U.S. agencies, African governments, and the private sector, noted as follows:

- *East Africa trade hub*, established in Nairobi, Kenya, in 2002. This hub aims to increase food security and economic growth in the following 9 East or Central African countries: Burundi, Ethiopia, Kenya, Madagascar, Mauritius, Rwanda, South Sudan, Tanzania, and Uganda.
- *West Africa trade hub*, established in Accra, Ghana, in 2003. This hub focuses on addressing critical issues that hamper export competitiveness such as high transport and telecommunications costs, limited access to finance, and inconsistent implementation of regional trade policies in 20 West African countries: Benin, Burkina Faso, Cameroon, Cape Verde, Chad, Côte d'Ivoire, Gabon, The Gambia, Ghana, Guinea, Guinea-Bissau,[29] Liberia, Mali, Mauritania, Niger, Nigeria, São Tomé and Príncipe, Senegal, Sierra Leone, and Togo.
- *Southern Africa trade hub*, established in Gaborone, Botswana, in 2004. This hub's primary goals are to increase international competitiveness, as well as intraregional trade and food security, by promoting greater competitiveness in agriculture value chains, increasing investment and export opportunities in the textile and apparel sector, and supporting a better business-enabling environment in 8 Southern African countries: Botswana, Lesotho, Malawi, Mozambique, Namibia, South Africa, Swaziland, and Zambia.

Along with implementing activities to support U.S. initiatives in areas such as food security, USAID-funded trade hubs seek to support trade facilitation, market linkages, and information awareness about AGOA to AGOA-exporting firms and countries. For example, from 2007 through 2012, USAID provided funding for activities implemented through the West Africa trade hub to address economy-wide constraints such as the transport and trade barriers affecting the region's ports, corridors, and borders. The trade hub established an advocacy campaign to address such trade barriers and help decrease the costs associated with trading. The trade hub also worked with governments in the region to establish border information centers that help stakeholders coordinate, and provide information and assistance to traders at borders to ease transport bottlenecks. The trade hub in East Africa has helped subsidize the cost to exporters of attending trade shows to gain exposure to U.S. markets in sectors including leather goods and apparel, and has facilitated U.S. buyers going to sub-Saharan Africa. Among its trade-related agriculture activities, the Southern Africa trade hub has provided training to medium- and large-scale commodity buyers and storage operators trading in maize and soybeans to help reduce postharvest loss and improve procurement practices.

Officials we spoke to in Ethiopia and Ghana cited some improvement in areas where USAID has provided TCB assistance while highlighting other ongoing challenges related to facilitating exports under AGOA. Although the West Africa trade hub began efforts in 2009 to help facilitate financial services for local companies, local business representatives from the cashew and shea industries in Ghana said lack of access to finance and the business community's lack of awareness on how to use AGOA remain challenges to utilizing AGOA. A representative of the horticulture industry in Ethiopia cited inefficient customs processes and lack of access to finance in the country as challenges to more fully utilizing AGOA. He also said that while certain logistical challenges had been addressed in terms of direct airline routes to the United States, increasing awareness of the Ethiopian flower industry would help improve access to the U.S. market. The owner of a textile goods company who had exported products under AGOA said he was unable to obtain certain inputs for his products in Ethiopia, a fact that affected decisions on what to produce. Furthermore, he said local businesses were rudimentary when AGOA was signed, and are only now building export capacity and an understanding of the U.S. market. A business representative from the apparel industry said that logistics remain a challenge to exports because of high transportation costs that may discourage potential buyers. He noted the high cost of moving shipments from Ethiopia to the port in Djibouti, and also that lengthy transport schedules create longer lead times to fill orders. Like other members of the private sector we spoke to, he said that local companies have limited access to capital, and that obtaining financing requires a number of bureaucratic steps.

USAID Has Worked with Some Host Governments on Strategic Approaches to AGOA Utilization, but Most Host Governments Have Not Established Such Approaches

USAID Has Worked with Some Host Governments to Develop Strategic Approaches to AGOA Utilization

USAID works with some host governments to develop strategic approaches to increasing AGOA utilization.[30] As previously noted, one of

USAID's core development objectives is to promote sustainable, broad-based economic growth by helping developing countries increase their exports through trade capacity building.

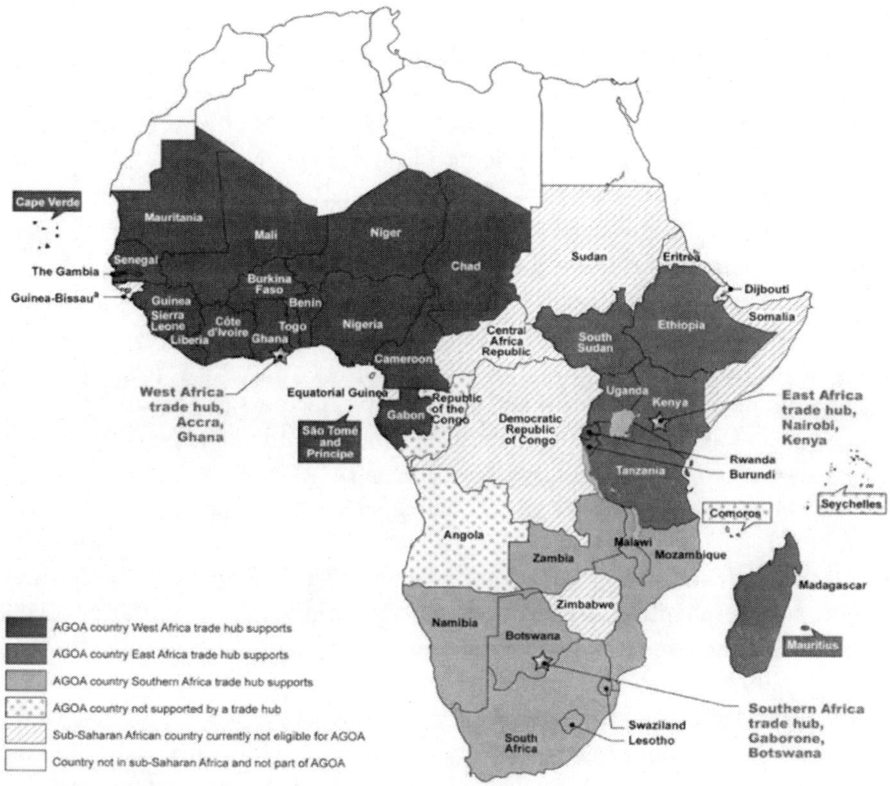

Soure: GAO analysis of USAID data, and Map Resources (map). | GAO-15-218.

[a]Although it was not eligible for the African Growth and Opportunity Act (AGOA) as of December 1, 2014, according to data from USAID, Guinea-Bissau was supported by the West Africa trade hub. On December 23, 2014, Guinea-Bissau was designated eligible for AGOA benefits.

Figure 6. Sub-Saharan African Countries Supported by USAID-Funded Regional Trade Hubs, as of December 2014.

AGOA legislation also directs the President, in part, to target assistance to sub-Saharan African governments. USAID has identified trade hubs as primary implementers of TCB assistance to African governments and organizations, among others. USAID, partly through the trade hubs, has supported AGOA utilization by collaborating with African governments to develop AGOAspecific or national export strategies. In the strategy documents, host governments may identify high-priority trade and investment sectors, constraints related to AGOA utilization, and specific steps to increase exports under AGOA. For example, the East Africa trade hub participated in a 2013 workshop with officials from the Mauritian government, and helped the host government develop and publish its AGOA-specific national strategy, which aims to support the ability of Mauritian firms to sell to the U.S. market and leverage opportunities that AGOA provides. Data from USAID also indicate that trade hubs provided input toward strategies that the Gambia and Senegal have developed.

We previously identified the importance of strategic planning efforts in results-oriented management.[31] Specifically, we found that such strategic planning efforts are the starting point and foundation for defining what the organization seeks to accomplish, and in identifying the strategies it will use to achieve desired results. Furthermore, developing a strategic plan can help clarify organizational priorities and unify staff in the pursuit of shared goals. If done well, strategic planning fosters informed communication between the organization and its stakeholders. In the case of AGOA utilization, this may include collaboration between U.S. and host governments, and the private sector.

Literature and trade hub reports have noted the potentially positive effects such strategies can have on countries' utilization of AGOA. USAID, through its trade hubs, has stated that identifying strategic needs and priorities through national strategies can bolster AGOA utilization. For example, in a 2013 report prepared for USAID, the West Africa trade hub noted the importance of a strategy as part of leveraging trade preferences, and the role that USAID and other U.S. agencies can play in encouraging strategy development. [32] The report identified several countries, including Burkina Faso and Sierra Leone, that have implemented strategies as tools to better utilize AGOA. Similarly, the East Africa trade hub reported that national strategies reflect host governments' strategic needs in approaching the U.S. market and outline ways governments can utilize AGOA. According to contractors who implement activities at one of the trade hubs, export strategies allow governments to target specific sectors and work with the private sector toward a unified approach.

African leaders have also articulated the importance of strategic approaches to enhancing AGOA utilization. At the 2011 AGOA Forum held in Zambia, an African trade minister underscored the importance of clear AGOA national strategies because they help ensure that countries assess export promotion challenges in a coordinated manner, and U.S. agency officials said that African leaders had committed to developing more AGOA-related strategies at the August 2014 Africa Leaders Summit. Furthermore, in a January 2014 testimony to USITC, a senior African official said AGOA countries have recognized the need to address various supply-side constraints that have hindered AGOA utilization, including poor infrastructure, by developing a coordinated, strategic response at the national level.[33] This official also noted that this strategic exercise would enable AGOA countries to identify supply-side constraints and potential responses, and may ultimately enable the U.S. government to better support African countries. For example, the Ethiopian government has drafted a national strategy that identifies high-priority industries that align with AGOA trade preferences. While this document is still in draft form, the Ethiopian trade ministry notes that its AGOA national strategy is an important part of the country's overall growth plan, given that AGOA is a useful market opportunity to achieve Ethiopia's larger economic growth objectives. According to officials, the government also plans to establish an AGOA center to oversee implementation of the strategy.

Most Host Governments Have Not Established a Strategic Approach to AGOA Utilization

Though USAID has made efforts to work with host governments on developing strategic approaches to AGOA utilization, 14 out of the 41 current AGOA countries have such strategies in place, according to data from USAID (see fig. 7). 34 According to a white paper from the United Nations Economic Commission for Africa and the African Union, the lack of a strategic approach on AGOA is a significant reason for gaps in AGOA utilization.[35] A 2011 Brookings Institution report[36] identified the lack of an AGOA national strategy as one factor inhibiting Ghana from fully benefitting from AGOA.[37]

According to officials and information from trade hubs, AGOA countries may lack these strategies because such efforts have not been prioritized in work plans, and because of an absence of political will among host governments. Specifically, in its work plans for all three trade hub contracts, USAID has noted the importance of coordinating with bilateral USAID missions, regional entities in sub-Saharan Africa, and host governments, among others.

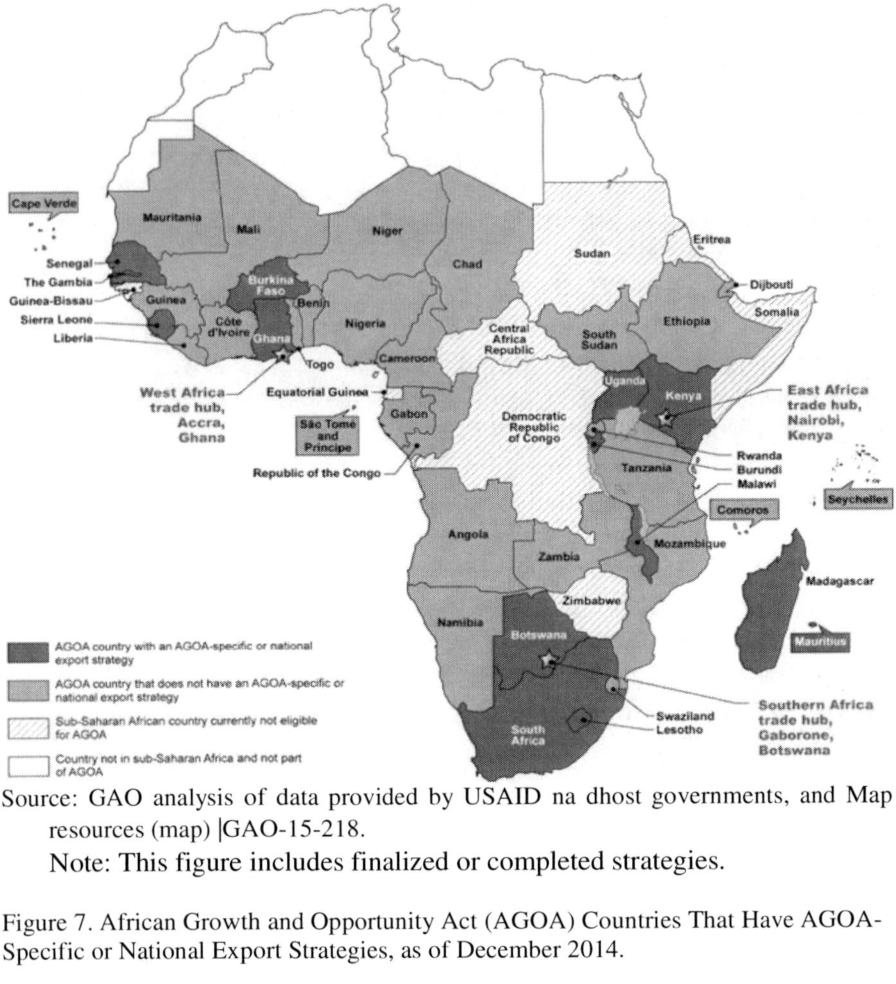

Source: GAO analysis of data provided by USAID na dhost governments, and Map resources (map) |GAO-15-218.

Note: This figure includes finalized or completed strategies.

Figure 7. African Growth and Opportunity Act (AGOA) Countries That Have AGOA-Specific or National Export Strategies, as of December 2014.

However, USAID only included the development of national strategies as a high-priority task for the East Africa trade hub, and not for the West and Southern Africa trade hubs. Furthermore, a lack of host government interest could influence the effectiveness of such efforts. A West Africa trade hub report noted that political will is needed to sustain strategy development efforts in those AGOA countries that lack such strategies. USAID officials also said that host governments must request and initiate the process of developing these strategies, and the lack of political will to motivate these efforts may be one reason some AGOA countries do not have such a strategic approach. For example, according to literature, some USAID TCB assistance programs in sub-Saharan Africa have faced challenges in gaining buy-in from regional participating governments and in ensuring agreement on the direction and pace of adoption of relevant processes and procedures. USAID officials acknowledged they could do more to work with host governments on strategy development to enhance AGOA utilization, and officials said they are starting to work with regional entities to develop strategic approaches to export promotion.

CONCLUSION

The U.S. government has acknowledged the importance of providing TCB assistance in support of AGOA, and U.S. agencies have obligated approximately $5 billion in TCB assistance for AGOA countries over a 13-year period. As Congress deliberates reauthorization of the AGOA program, policymakers have expressed interest in enhancing eligible countries' ability to utilize the program and ensuring that TCB assistance is aligned with the program's objectives. A strategic approach to AGOA utilization can help eligible countries leverage U.S. TCB efforts and trade preferences under AGOA, while a lack of a strategic approach to AGOA can result in gaps in program utilization. Although USAID has worked with some host governments from AGOA countries to develop strategic approaches to program utilization, about a third of the 41 AGOA countries currently have strategies that reflect AGOA priorities. USAID has not prioritized the development of these strategies for all three of its regional trade hubs, which play a significant role in implementing TCB in AGOA countries and working with host governments. A lack of political will among host governments may also pose challenges to developing and sustaining strategic approaches related to AGOA. In developing these approaches, eligible countries can identify trade barriers that inhibit AGOA utilization and articulate a commitment to addressing these barriers. Such strategies could also assist U.S. agencies in ensuring that TCB assistance is aligned with host government priorities and is addressing gaps in AGOA utilization.

Recommendation for Executive Action

To enhance eligible countries' ability to utilize the AGOA program and ensure that TCB assistance is aligned with program objectives, we recommend that the Administrator of USAID work with more host governments to develop strategic approaches to promoting exports under AGOA

Agency Comments and Our Evaluation

USAID stated that it agreed with the report's overall findings, conclusions, and recommendations. USAID also made a number of observations and comments related to the findings and recommendation in the report.

USAID commented that our report does not provide sufficient data to demonstrate the linkage between host government strategic approaches and AGOA utilization. However, as we point out in our report, such strategies can have potentially positive effects on countries' utilization of AGOA. We cite prior GAO work that notes the importance of strategic planning efforts in results-oriented management; and literature, trade hub reports, and statements from African leaders that also emphasize the importance of strategic approaches to enhancing AGOA utilization.

USAID stated that our report does not include the point that the productivity of African businesses is negatively impacted by a lack of access to reliable electricity. However, our report does in fact note observations from our field work in Ghana and Ethiopia regarding challenges resulting from lack of access to power.

Finally, USAID explained that its trade hubs are designed as regional programs and therefore often prioritize regional efforts over bilateral strategy development. In our report we acknowledge the regional focus of USAID-funded trade hubs and also note that USAID is starting to work with regional entities to develop strategic approaches to export promotion.

Commerce, State, the Treasury, MCC, USITC, and USTR also received a draft copy of the report but did not provide formal comments. USAID, USITC, and USTR provided technical comments, which we have incorporated in the report, as appropriate.

Kimberly Gianopoulos, Director, International Affairs and Trade.

APPENDIX I: OBJECTIVES, SCOPE, AND METHODOLOGY

Our objectives were to examine (1) U.S. government trade capacity building (TCB) assistance in support of the African Growth and Opportunity Act (AGOA), and (2) the extent to which the U.S. Agency for International Development (USAID) has made efforts to develop strategic approaches to AGOA utilization.

To address both objectives, we interviewed officials from the Departments of Commerce, State, and the Treasury; the Millennium Challenge Corporation (MCC); and USAID, but focused on MCC and USAID for the purposes of this report because these agencies obligated the highest amounts of TCB funding from fiscal years 2001 through 2013. We also interviewed officials from the Office of the U.S. Trade Representative and the U.S. International Trade Commission (USITC), agencies that do not provide funding for U.S. TCB assistance but provided additional contextual information on AGOA and TCB. We reviewed documents including literature on AGOA and TCB; statements of work, evaluations, and annual reports for the three USAID-funded trade hubs; program documents for MCC activities in sub-Saharan Africa; and examples of AGOA-specific and national export strategies. We also conducted fieldwork in Ethiopia and Ghana, countries we selected because they represented a cross section of U.S. TCB assistance and are in different regions within sub-Saharan Africa, thereby also providing insight on two out of the three trade hubs. In each country, we interviewed U.S. agency officials, host government officials, representatives from the private sector who had insights on U.S. TCB assistance, and contractors implementing TCB activities. Our findings from these countries are not generalizable to the universe of all U.S. TCB activities.

To examine U.S. government TCB assistance in support of AGOA, we reviewed documents from relevant U.S. agencies, including program descriptions and evaluations, and analyzed data on U.S. TCB funding to AGOA countries. We focused our analysis on the U.S. agencies that provided the highest amounts of TCB funding for AGOA countries from fiscal years 2001 through 2013. We analyzed data USAID provided on annual U.S. TCB obligations for activities in all AGOA countries from fiscal years 2001 through 2013 by year, agency, country, and TCB category. These data are reported in the U.S. government TCB database, but we requested data directly from USAID to facilitate our analysis of the data for the purposes of this report. We also relied on the data and information from the TCB database, such as TCB activity descriptions. In our analysis of TCB funding data, we built upon information collected for prior GAO reports on TCB that used data from the

TCB database.[1] Data from the TCB database were deemed reliable for our prior reports on TCB.[2] For this report, we determined that the data were sufficiently reliable to identify TCB funding by agency, country, category, and year. Furthermore, in assessing the data, we interviewed key USAID officials responsible for administering the database and reviewed supporting documentation.

To examine the extent to which USAID has made efforts to develop strategic approaches to AGOA utilization, we reviewed documents from relevant U.S. agencies, including program descriptions and evaluations, and information on AGOA-specific and national export strategies from U.S. agencies and host governments. In addition, we discussed the development of these strategic approaches with U.S. and foreign government officials.

We conducted this performance audit from March 2014 to January 2015 in accordance with generally accepted government auditing standards. Those standards require that we plan and perform the audit to obtain sufficient, appropriate evidence to provide a reasonable basis for our findings and conclusions based on our audit objectives. We believe that the evidence obtained provides a reasonable basis for our findings and conclusions based on our audit objectives.

Appendix II: U.S. Government Trade Capacity Building (TCB) Database Definitional Categories and Examples of Activities in African Growth and Opportunity Act (AGOA) Countries

As we noted in 2011, the U.S. Agency for International Development (USAID) collects data to identify and quantify the U.S. government's trade capacity building (TCB) activities in developing countries through an annual survey of U.S. agencies.[1]

TCB Category Definitions

The U.S. government TCB database defines the categories as follows:

- World Trade Organization (WTO) Accession and Compliance: support for countries to benefit from membership in the WTO, or to understand fully the benefits of membership. Also assistance to help countries in the WTO accession process meet the requirements of accession. This category includes assistance to meet the obligations of the specific WTO agreements, except for Agreements on Sanitary and Phyto-Sanitary Measures (SPS), Technical Barriers to Trade (TBT), Intellectual Property Rights (IPR), and Trade-related Procurement. Those four agreements benefit from TCB in their own categories.

- Sanitary and Phyto-Sanitary Measures: support for countries to meet SPS standards for trade and to comply with the WTO Agreement on SPS.
- Technical Barriers to Trade: support for countries to reduce technical barriers to trade and to comply with the WTO Agreement on TBT.
- Intellectual Property Rights: support for countries to observe international standards on intellectual property rights protection and to comply with the WTO Agreement on IPR.
- Trade-Related Procurement: support for increased trade related to government procurement and to comply with the WTO Agreement on Government Procurement.
- Trade Facilitation: generally defined as assistance in lowering the costs of engaging in, or eliminating obstacles to, international trade flows. Trade facilitation (for 2011) is a sum of the following four subcategories:
  - Customs Operations: includes assistance to help countries modernize and improve their customs offices.
  - Trade Promotion: includes assistance to increase market opportunities for developing country and transition economy producers.
  - Enterprise Development: includes support to improve the associations and networks in the business sector, as well as to enhance the skills of business people engaged in trade. Also includes assistance to help countries acquire and use information technology to promote trade by creating business networks and disseminating market information.
  - Free Trade Agreements (FTA) and Trade Integration: includes assistance to an FTA, a regional trade agreement (RTA), or an individual country that increases the ability of the RTA to facilitate trade. It can also include assistance to a potential member of an RTA that improves the analytical capacity of the country's government with respect to RTA issues.[2]

- Trade-Related Labor: assistance to support the enforcement of labor standards and worker rights, development of trade unions and dispute resolution mechanisms, strategies for workforce development and worker training, and the elimination of child labor.
- Financial Sector: support for financial sector work, monetary and fiscal policy, exchange rates, commodity markets, and capital markets.
- Trade-Related Infrastructure: assistance to establish trade-related telecoms, transport, ports, airports, power, water, and industrial zones.
- Environmental Sector Trade and Standards: assistance to establish environmental standards or to promote environmental technology.
- Competition Policy, Business Environment, and Governance: support for the design and implementation of antitrust laws, as well as of laws and regulations related to investment and investor protections. Includes support for legal and institutional reform to improve governance and make policies more transparent, and assistance to help the different agencies of a host country government function more effectively in the trade policy arena.
- Trade-Related Agriculture: support for trade-related aspects of the agriculture and agribusiness sectors.[3]
- Trade-Related Services: includes support to help developing countries and transition economies increase their flows of trade in services. Services Trade Development is a sum of two subcategories:
    - Trade-Related Services (excluding tourism): assistance to help countries develop trade in services in all sectors other than tourism, including financial services, energy, transportation, and education.
    - Trade-Related Tourism: assistance to help countries expand their international tourism sectors, including eco-tourism.
- Other Trade Capacity Building: A small number of TCB activities did not fit in any of the above categories, including some activities of a crosscutting nature. These were categorized as "Other Trade Capacity Building."

Table 4. Examples of U.S. Trade Capacity Building (TCB) Assistance Activities in African Growth and Opportunity Act (AGOA) Countries, by TCB Assistance Category

TCB category	U.S. TCB assistance activities in AGOA countries
World Trade Organization (WTO) accession and compliance	In Ethiopia, the U.S. government supported a WTO accession project that aimed to promote policy and legal reform to help bring the country's trade regime into line with WTO rules; build political, public, and private sector support for accession; and develop institutional capacity within the government to analyze trade policy measures.
Sanitary and phyto-sanitary measures	In Burkina Faso, the U.S. government provided technical assistance to the Ministry of Commerce that aimed to improve the country's sanitary and phyto-sanitary inspection and compliance regime.
Technical barriers to trade	In Zambia, the U.S. government supported a project that aimed to reduce barriers to trade and investment through assistance for a small-claims court system. This project aimed to assist in the speedy resolution of internal trade disputes and increase capacity for external trade.
Intellectual property rights	In Liberia, the U.S. government supported the development and implementation of an intellectual property policy framework, strengthening of enforcement, and provision of training to educate relevant stakeholders.
Trade-related procurement	In South Sudan, the U.S. government provided assistance to the Ministry of Petroleum to increase petroleum exports and nonpetroleum exports, and helped ensure that the country's fiscal policies provided business-friendly tax structures.
Trade facilitation	In Burundi, U.S. government assistance aimed to diversify rural economic opportunities and strengthen trade capacity through technical and trade promotional assistance to producers and small- and medium-sized enterprises in the coffee, horticulture, and dairy sectors.
Trade-related labor	In Lesotho, the U.S. government supported improvements in enterprises' adherence to international core labor standards and national labor law, enabling these enterprises to compete in global markets.
Financial sector	In Ghana, the U.S. government provided assistance to the Ministry of Finance to establish a debt management unit, ensuring domestic debt sustainability and coordination between the ministry and the Bank of Ghana.
Trade-related infrastructure	In Benin, the U.S. government supported assistance to improve port performance and security, expand capacity, and reduce costs. Assistance also focused on reducing delays at the port and increasing the volume of imports and exports.

Table 4. (Continued)

TCB category	U.S. TCB assistance activities in AGOA countries
Environmental sector trade and standards	In Malawi, the U.S. government provided assistance to community-based natural resource management initiatives that generate income and provide incentives for sustainable resource use and biodiversity conservation.
Competition policy, business environment, and governance	In Tanzania, the U.S. government provided assistance to technical services that aimed to improve the country's economic performance. Areas covered include agribusiness diagnostics, private sector health diagnostics, and women-focused research and reforms.
Trade-related agriculture	In Kenya, the U.S. government provided assistance to a horticulture development program that aimed to increase smallholder farmers' incomes through market growth, enhancements of U.S.-Kenya trade, and support for tree crops.
Trade-related services	In Madagascar, U.S. government assistance for a forest ecosystems conservation program promoted natural products such as medicinal plants and spices, and ecotourism developmentthrough training tour operators.
Other trade capacity building	In Nigeria, the U.S. government provided support for customs reform and modernization, transport corridor improvements, and trade capacity building.

Source: GAO analysis of data from the U.S. government TCB database. | GAO-15-218.

End Notes

[1] AGOA was originally enacted as Pub. L. No. 106-200, May 18, 2000. Since its enactment, AGOA has been amended three times, by Pub. L. No. 107-210, August 6, 2002; Pub. L. No. 108-274, July 12, 2004; and Pub. L. No. 109-432, December 20, 2006.

[2] Trade preference programs offer unilateral tariff reductions to eligible developing countries for the import of specified products into the United States. AGOA authorizes the President to designate countries as eligible to receive AGOA program benefits if they are determined to have met certain criteria, including having established, or made continual progress toward establishing, market-based economies; the rule of law and political pluralism; elimination of barriers to U.S. trade and investment; protection of intellectual property; systems to combat corruption; policies to reduce poverty and increase availability of health care and educational opportunities; and protection of human rights and worker rights, including elimination of certain child labor practices. In addition, the President must determine that countries have not engaged in activities that undermine U.S. national security or foreign policy interests, and do not engage in gross violations of human rights or provide support for acts of terrorism.

[3] We previously reported that from 2001 to 2008, total U.S. imports from these countries, including imports under AGOA, grew from $20 billion to $82 billion, an increase of 300 percent. However, since 2008, total imports have decreased by 53 percent. Since 2008, U.S. imports under AGOA have declined from $56 billion to $25 billion, a decrease of 56 percent. See GAO, African Growth and Opportunity Act: Observations on Competitiveness and Diversification of U.S. Imports from Beneficiary Countries, GAO-14-722R (Washington, D.C.: July 21, 2014).

[4] TCB broadly describes assistance that positively affects a country's ability to secure benefits from international trade. See GAO, Foreign Assistance: USAID Should Update Its Trade Capacity Building Strategy, GAO-14-602 (Washington, D.C.: Sept. 10, 2014); Foreign Assistance: The United States Provides Wide-ranging Trade Capacity Building Assistance, but Better Reporting and Evaluation Are Needed, GAO-11-727 (Washington, D.C.: July 29, 2011); and Foreign Assistance: U.S. Trade Capacity Building Extensive, but Its Effectiveness Has Yet to Be Evaluated, GAO-05-150 (Washington, D.C.: Feb. 11, 2005).

[5] White House, "Presidential Memorandum–Establishing a Comprehensive Approach to Expanding Sub-Saharan Africa's Capacity for Trade and Investment" (August 2014), accessed August 5, 2014, http://www.whitehouse.gov/the-press-office/2014/08/04/presidential-memorandum-establishing-comprehensive-approach-expanding-su.

[6] In GAO-14-602, we recommended that the Administrator of USAID update USAID's 2003 TCB strategy to reflect the current TCB operating environment.

[7] In December 2013 during the 113th Congress, various committees and subcommittees asked us to review a number of issues as AGOA comes up for renewal in 2015. These committees and subcommittees included the Chairmen and Ranking Members of the Senate Finance Committee; the Senate Foreign Relations Committee; the Senate Finance Subcommittee on International Trade, Customs, and Global Competiveness; the Senate Foreign Relations Subcommittee on African Affairs; the House Foreign Affairs Committee; the House Ways and Means Committee; the House Foreign Affairs Subcommittee on Africa, Global Health, Global Human Rights, and International Organizations; and the House Ways and Means Subcommittee on Trade.

[8] GAO-14-722R.

[9] According to USITC, one way to define AGOA utilization is U.S. imports under AGOA from an AGOA country as a share of total U.S. imports from that country. See J. Bonarriva and J. Guth, AGOA: Trade and Investment Performance Overview, United States International Trade Commission Publication Number: 4461 (United States International Trade Commission, Washington, DC: April 2014).

[10] The United States has offered tariff reductions for goods from most sub-Saharan African countries under the Generalized System of Preferences (GSP). The Africa Investment Incentive Act of 2006, Pub. L. No. 109-432, div. D, Title VI, expanded the list of products that eligible sub-Saharan African countries may export to the United States duty-free under GSP, which covers approximately 4,600 items. GSP and AGOA eligibility criteria overlap, and countries must be GSP eligible to take advantage of trade benefits under AGOA. Though legal authorization of the GSP program expired on July 31, 2013, GSPeligible imports from AGOA countries will continue to be eligible for duty-free entry, pursuant to the provisions of the statute governing the AGOA program.

[11] AGOA contains a list of countries that are potentially eligible for AGOA benefits and authorizes the President to designate countries as eligible to receive such benefits if the President determines that they have met, or are making continual progress toward meeting,

a set base of requirements, such as the rule of law and political pluralism and protection of human rights and workers rights.

[12] For the purposes of this report, we defined AGOA countries as the group of 41 countries that were eligible for AGOA benefits as of December 1, 2014. The 41 AGOA countries included in this report are Angola, Benin, Botswana, Burkina Faso, Burundi, Cameroon, Cape Verde, Chad, Comoros, Republic of Congo, Côte d'Ivoire, Djibouti, Ethiopia, Gabon, the Gambia, Ghana, Guinea, Kenya, Lesotho, Liberia, Madagascar, Malawi, Mali, Mauritania, Mauritius, Mozambique, Namibia, Niger, Nigeria, Rwanda, São Tomé and Príncipe, Senegal, Seychelles, Sierra Leone, South Africa, South Sudan, Swaziland, Tanzania, Togo, Uganda, and Zambia. As of December 1, 2014, The eight countries in sub-Saharan Africa that are not currently eligible for AGOA benefits are Central African Republic, Democratic Republic of Congo, Equatorial Guinea, Eritrea, Guinea-Bissau, Somalia, Sudan, and Zimbabwe were not eligible for AGOA benefits. See figure 6 for a map of sub-Saharan Africa that indicates AGOA countries for the purposes of this report. On December 23, 2014, Guinea-Bissau was designated eligible for AGOA benefits. Effective January 1, 2015, the Gambia, South Sudan, and Swaziland were no longer designated eligible for AGOA benefits.

[13] AGOA legislation also directs the President to develop and implement policies to encourage investment in eligible sub-Saharan African countries with a particular focus on infrastructure, information and communication technology, and agriculture processing and capacity enhancement.

[14] According to the U.S. Trade and Development Agency (USTDA), reverse trade missions bring foreign buyers to the United States in order to observe the design, manufacture, demonstration and operation of U.S. products and services that can help them achieve their development goals.

[15] Trade in services refers to the buying and selling of intangible products and activities; examples of trade-in-services sectors include tourism, financial services, and telecommunications. See GAO, Sub-Saharan Africa: Trends in U.S. and Chinese Economic Engagement, GAO-13-199 (Washington, D.C.: Feb. 7, 2013).

[16] International Finance Corporation, Access to Finance: Sub-Saharan Africa (Johannesburg, South Africa: World Bank Group, 2013).

[17] Congressional Research Service, African Growth and Opportunity Act (AGOA): Background and Reauthorization (Washington, D.C.: July 24, 2014).

[18] Bonarriva and Guth, AGOA: Trade and Investment Performance Overview (United States International Trade Commission Publication Number: 4461).

[19] GAO-14-602.

[20] In January 2004, Congress established MCC to administer the Millennium Challenge Account for foreign assistance. MCC's mission is to reduce poverty by supporting sustainable, transformative economic growth in partnership with developing countries that create and maintain sound policy environments. MCC signs compacts obligating funds for such projects with countries it selects as eligible for this assistance, according to criteria outlined in MCC's authorizing legislation.

[21] GAO-14-602.

[22] MCC's TCB assistance in AGOA countries has covered the following 10 TCB categories: competition policy, business environment, and governance; environmental standards and trade; financial sector; intellectual property rights; trade facilitation; trade-related agriculture; trade-related infrastructure; trade-related services; WTO accession and compliance; and other TCB. MCC did not provide assistance in the following 4 TCB

categories: sanitary and phyto-sanitary measures, technical barriers to trade, trade-related labor, and trade-related procurement.

[23] In August 2014, MCC signed a second compact with Ghana for about $498 million to create a financially viable power sector to address the needs of households and businesses.

[24] A partnership among the U.S. government, African governments, the private sector, and others, Power Africa aims to expand access to electricity to households and businesses and increase Africa's global competitiveness.

[25] The 12 government agencies supporting Power Africa are the Departments of Agriculture, Commerce, Energy, State, and the Treasury; the Export-Import Bank; MCC; the Overseas Private Investment Corporation; U.S. African Development Foundation; USAID; U.S. Army Corps of Engineers; and USTDA.

[26] Trade Africa includes efforts to form public-private partnerships to stimulate greater trade in goods under AGOA that incorporate the promotion of investment in trade-related infrastructure, among many other efforts.

[27] In addition to providing funding for 39 individual countries, USAID also provided funding for sub-Saharan Africa under regional groupings, such as East and Central Africa, Western Africa, and Southern Africa.

[28] Although they are AGOA-eligible countries, Angola, Comoros, Republic of Congo, Djibouti, and Seychelles are not covered by any of the trade hubs.

[29] Although it was not eligible for AGOA as of December 1, 2014, according to data from USAID, Guinea-Bissau was supported by the West Africa trade hub. On December 23, 2014, Guinea-Bissau was designated eligible for AGOA benefits.

[30] According to USITC, in 2013, AGOA utilization was 65 percent for trade in all products and across all countries. When crude petroleum imports are excluded from the calculation, the overall utilization rate falls to 31 percent. J. Bonarriva and J. Guth, AGOA: Trade and Investment Performance Overview.

[31] GAO, Agencies' Strategic Plans Under GPRA: Key Questions to Facilitate Congressional Review, GAO/GGD-10.1.16 (Washington, D.C.: May 1997).

[32] CARANA Corporation, West Africa Trade Hub Final Report, a report prepared at the request of USAID, August 2013.

[33] This testimony was provided at a public hearing held in conjunction with USITC's AGOA reports. U.S. International Trade Commission, AGOA: Trade and Investment Performance Overview; AGOA: Economic Effects of Providing Duty-Free Treatment for Imports; U.S. AGOA Rules of Origin: Possible Changes to Promote Regional Integration and Increase Exports to the United States Performance Overview; EU—South Africa FTA: Impact on U.S. Exports to South Africa (Investigation Numbers 332-542, 332-544, 332-545, and 332-546) (Heritage Reporting Corporation, Washington, D.C.: Jan. 14, 2014).

[34] According to data from USAID, the 14 countries that had an AGOA-specific or national export strategy as of December 2014 were Botswana, Burkina Faso, Burundi, the Gambia, Ghana, Kenya, Lesotho, Madagascar, Malawi, Mauritius, Senegal, Sierra Leone, South Africa, and Uganda.

[35] United Nations Economic Commission for Africa and the African Union, How 'AGOA 2.0.' Could Be Different: Outlining Africa's Position on the AGOA Review Process (Addis Ababa, Ethiopia: April 2014).

[36] Elizabeth A. Asante, Simon Bawakyillenuo, and Clement Ahiadeke. Brookings Institution, Improving AGOA: Toward a New Framework for U.S.-Africa Commercial Engagement (Washington, D.C.: May 2011).

[37] Ghana issued national export strategies in 2013, and Ghanaian government officials said they were taking steps to develop an implementation plan for those strategies.

End Notes for Appendix I

[1] GAO, Foreign Assistance: USAID Should Update Its Trade Capacity Building Strategy, GAO-14-602 (Washington, D.C.: Sept. 10, 2014); Foreign Assistance: The United States Provides Wide-ranging Trade Capacity Building Assistance, but Better Reporting and Evaluation Are Needed, GAO-11-727 (Washington, D.C.: July 29, 2011); and Foreign Assistance: U.S. Trade Capacity Building Extensive, but Its Effectiveness Has Yet to Be Evaluated, GAO-05-150 (Washington, D.C.: Feb. 11, 2005).

[2] We identified limitations to the TCB database in our 2011 report on TCB, including that the database did not adequately explain significant factors driving changes in the composition of TCB funding over time.

End Notes for Appendix II

[1] GAO-11-727, 4-5.

[2] This category does not include TCB assistance in a specific area that is being provided to countries through an RTA. For example, technical assistance to help RTA member countries comply with SPS standards was reported as Trade-Related Agricultural Development or the WTO Agreement on SPS Measures.

[3] Support that is specifically intended to help countries participate in the WTO Agreements on Agriculture or SPS Measures is not included in this category.

In: African Growth and Opportunity Act
Editor: Hellen Edwards
ISBN: 978-1-63482-981-6

Chapter 2

AFRICAN GROWTH AND OPPORTUNITY ACT: ELIGIBILITY PROCESS AND ECONOMIC DEVELOPMENT IN SUB-SAHARAN AFRICA*

United States Government Accountability Office

WHY GAO DID THIS STUDY

Enacted in 2000 and set to expire in September 2015, AGOA is a trade preference program that seeks to promote economic development in 49 sub-Saharan African countries by allowing eligible countries to export qualifying goods to the United States without import duties. The act requires the U.S. government to conduct an annual eligibility review to assess each country's progress on economic, political, and development reform objectives in order to be eligible for AGOA benefits. AGOA also requires an annual forum to foster closer economic ties between the United States and sub-Saharan African countries.

GAO was asked to review various issues related to AGOA's economic development benefits. In this report, GAO examines (1) how the AGOA eligibility review process has considered economic, political, and development reform objectives described in the act and (2) how sub-Saharan African

* This is an edited, reformatted and augmented version of a United States Government Accountability Office publication, No. GAO-15-300, dated February 2015.

countries have fared in certain economic development outcomes since the enactment of AGOA.

GAO reviewed documents and interviewed officials from U.S. agencies to examine the relationship between the U.S. government's review process and AGOA reform criteria. GAO analyzed trends in economic development indicators for AGOA eligible and ineligible countries from 2001 to 2012, the latest year for which data were available for most countries.

WHAT GAO RECOMMENDS

GAO is not making any recommendations.

WHAT GAO FOUND

The U.S. government uses the annual eligibility review process required by the African Growth and Opportunity Act (AGOA) to engage with sub-Saharan African countries on their progress toward economic, political, and development reform objectives reflected in AGOA's eligibility criteria. Managed by the Office of the United States Trade Representative, the review process brings together officials from U.S. agencies each year to discuss the progress each country is making with regard to AGOA's eligibility criteria and to reach consensus as to which countries should be deemed eligible to receive AGOA benefits. Over the lifetime of AGOA, 13 countries have lost AGOA eligibility, although 7 eventually had it restored (see figure). To encourage reforms, the U.S. government will engage with countries experiencing difficulty meeting eligibility criteria and may specify measures a country can take. For example, U.S. officials met with Swaziland officials over several years to discuss steps to improve labor rights. However, Swaziland did not make the necessary reforms and lost eligibility effective in January 2015.

GAO analyzed data on economic development indicators for sub-Saharan African countries that were eligible and ineligible for AGOA in 2012; the results showed that eligible countries fared better than ineligible countries on some economic measures since the enactment of AGOA. The extent to which this outcome is attributable to AGOA, however, is difficult to isolate after additional factors are taken into consideration. Other factors, such as the small share of AGOA exports in the overall exports of many AGOA-eligible countries, the role of petroleum exports in recent income growth, the quality of government institutions, and differences in levels of foreign aid and investment, make it difficult to isolate AGOA's contribution to overall economic development. For example, AGOA exports are a small share of overall exports for the majority of AGOA-eligible countries. GAO found evidence that increasing energy prices may also have contributed to income growth within AGOA-eligible petroleum-exporting countries. GAO also found that AGOA-eligible countries on average had higher governance scores and received more foreign aid and investment compared with ineligible countries. These differences may have contributed to economic development in AGOA-eligible countries, but they may also have been facilitated by AGOA, a possibility that makes it difficult to isolate AGOA's impact on economic development.

Eligibility lost and not regained	Reason for losing eligibility	Eligibility lost and regained	Reason for losing eligibility
• Central African Republic	• Coup	• Côte d'Ivoire	• Political unrest and armed conflict
• Democratic Republic of Congo	• Human rights abuses	• Guinea	• Coup
• Eritrea	• Human rights abuses	• Guinea-Bissau	• Coup
• The Gambia	• Human rights abuses	• Madagascar	• Coup
• South Sudan	• Political violence and armed conflict	• Mali	• Coup
		• Mauritania	• Coup
• Swaziland	• Labor rights	• Niger	• Rule of law

Source: GAO analysis of information from the Office of the U.S. Trade Representative. | GAO-15-300.

Thirteen Sub-Saharan African Countries That Lost Eligibility for Benefits under the African Growth and Opportunity Act and Their Current Eligibility Status.

Abbreviations

AGOA	African Growth and Opportunity Act
CPA	country programmable aid
FDI	foreign direct investment
GDP	gross domestic product
GSP	Generalized System of Preferences
ODA	official development assistance
OECD	Organisation for Economic Co-operation and Development
SSA	sub-Saharan Africa
TPSC	Trade Policy Staff Committee

USAID U.S. Agency for International Development
USTR Office of the U.S. Trade Representative

* * *

February 12, 2015

Congressional Requesters

Enacted in 2000, the African Growth and Opportunity Act (AGOA) seeks to promote economic development in 49 sub-Saharan African (SSA) countries by offering eligible countries enhanced trade preferences and encouraging the elimination of trade barriers in those countries.[1] AGOA is a U.S. trade preference program that allows eligible SSA countries to export qualifying goods to the United States without import duties. AGOA is intended to promote free markets, stimulate economic development in sub-Saharan Africa through export-led growth, and facilitate sub-Saharan Africa's integration into the global economy. The act requires the U.S. government to conduct an annual eligibility review to determine whether a country is making progress on economic, political, and development reform objectives described in the act in order to be eligible for AGOA benefits. AGOA also requires an annual forum that brings together representatives of the United States and SSA countries to foster closer economic ties.

With AGOA set to expire after September 30, 2015, we were asked to examine a number of issues relating to AGOA countries' trade expansion, economic development, and factors affecting their trade with the United States and other countries. In this report, the third in a series responding to your request, we examine (1) how the AGOA eligibility review process has considered and the AGOA Forums have supported economic, political, and development reform objectives described in the act and (2) how sub-Saharan African countries have fared in certain economic development outcomes since the enactment of AGOA.[2]

To examine how the U.S. government's process for determining AGOA eligibility and the AGOA Forums have supported reform objectives established in sections 104 and 105 of the act, we reviewed AGOA legislation and documents from the U.S. agencies that were relevant to the AGOA eligibility criteria and the AGOA Forums. We also analyzed the AGOA eligibility status for SSA countries since AGOA's original enactment to identify changes in eligibility from 2000 through January 2015. We also attended and observed 2014 AGOA Forum events. For both objectives, we interviewed officials from the Departments of Agriculture, Commerce, Labor, State, and the Treasury; the U.S. Agency for International Development (USAID); and the Office of the U.S. Trade Representative (USTR). These seven U.S. agencies are members of the AGOA Implementation Subcommittee of the Trade Policy Staff Committee (TPSC), and they provide reports on the sub-Saharan African countries for consideration during the annual eligibility review.[3]

To examine the relationship between AGOA eligibility and economic development in sub-Saharan Africa, we analyzed data on economic measures and indicators related to economic development, primarily consisting of the World Bank World Development Indicators, World Bank Worldwide Governance indicators, U.S. Census trade data, International Monetary Fund trade data, and Organisation for Economic Co-operation, and Development (OECD) data on foreign assistance. To assess the reliability of these data, we reviewed publicly available documents on these databases and conducted electronic testing for missing values and outliers. We determined that these data were sufficiently reliable for our purposes. We analyzed trends in selected economic development indicators for SSA countries since AGOA was first implemented and compared these trends across different groups of countries based on AGOA eligibility status. For most of this analysis, we used the AGOA eligibility status of SSA countries at the end of 2012 because that is the most recent year for which data are available in the April 2014 edition of the World Development Indicators to examine changes in economic development across SSA countries. We refer to the 40 SSA countries that were eligible for AGOA benefits at the end of 2012 as AGOA-eligible countries and the 9 countries that were not deemed eligible that year as AGOA-ineligible countries.[4] However, in our analysis of the AGOA share of overall exports, we use year 2013 export data and the list of AGOAeligible countries in 2013. Appendix I provides a detailed discussion of our objectives, scope, and methodology.

We conducted this performance audit from April 2014 to February 2015 in accordance with generally accepted government auditing standards. Those standards require that we plan and perform the audit to obtain sufficient, appropriate evidence to provide a reasonable basis for our findings and conclusions based on our audit objectives. We believe that the evidence obtained provides a reasonable basis for our findings and conclusions based on our audit objectives.

BACKGROUND

AGOA Benefits, Reform Objectives, and Eligibility Requirements

AGOA provides eligible SSA countries duty-free access to U.S. markets for more than 6,000 dutiable items in the U.S. import tariff schedules. SSA countries are defined in Section 107 of AGOA as the 49 sub-Saharan African countries potentially eligible for AGOA benefits listed in that provision. As a trade preference program, AGOA supports economic development in sub-Saharan Africa through trade and investment and encourages increased trade and investment between the United States and SSA countries as well as intra-SSA trade. In addition, AGOA benefits may lead to improved access to U.S. credit and technical assistance, according to the Department of Commerce's website and officials from the Departments of Commerce and Labor. AGOA authorizes the President each year to designate an SSA country as eligible for AGOA trade preferences if the President determines that the country has met or is making continual progress toward meeting AGOA's eligibility criteria, among other requirements.[5] For the purposes of this report, we have organized the act's eligibility criteria into three broad reform objectives: economic, political, and development (see table 1).

Table 1. Reform Objectives Related to Eligibility Criteria in the African Growth and Opportunity Act (AGOA)

Reform objective	AGOA eligibility criteria	
	Each country under review must show that it has established or is making continual progress toward establishing each of the following conditions:	Each country under review must also:
Economic	• A market-based economy that protects private property rights, incorporates an open rules-based trading system, and minimizes government interference in the economy through measures such as price controls, subsidies, and government ownership of economic assets. • The elimination of barriers to U.S. trade and investment, including by	

Reform objective	AGOA eligibility criteria	
	• the provision of national treatment and measures to create an environment conducive to domestic and foreign investment, • the protection of intellectual property, and • the resolution of bilateral trade and investment disputes.	
Political	• The rule of law; political pluralism; and the right to due process, a fair trial, and equal protection under the law. • A system to combat corruption and bribery, such as signing and implementing the Convention on Combating Bribery of Foreign Public Officials in International Business Transactions. • Protection of internationally recognized labor rights, including the right of association; the right to organize and bargain collectively; a prohibition on the use of any form of forced or compulsory labor; a minimum age for the employment of children; and acceptable conditions of work with respect to minimum wages, hours of work, and occupational safety and health.	• Not engage in activities that undermine U.S. national security or foreign policy interests. • Not engage in gross violations of internationally recognized human rights. • Not provide support for acts of international terrorism. • Cooperate in international efforts to eliminate human rights violations and terrorist activities. • Have implemented its commitments to eliminate the worst forms of child labor.
Developme nt	• Economic policies to reduce poverty, increase the availability of health care and educational opportunities, expand physical infrastructure, promote the development of private enterprise, and encourage the formation of capital markets through micro-credit or other programs.	

Source: GAO analysis of AGOA legislation. | GAO-15-300.

Note: For the purposes of this report, we have organized the act's eligibility criteria into three broad reform objectives: economic, political, and development.

In addition, the act requires that an SSA country be eligible for the Generalized System of Preferences (GSP) in order to be considered for AGOA benefits.[6] The U.S. government's *African Growth and Opportunity Act Implementation Guide* states that an SSA country must also officially request to be considered for AGOA benefits.[7] Over the lifetime of AGOA, 47 of the 49 SSA countries listed in the act have requested consideration for AGOA eligibility, according to USTR officials.[8] Figure 1 shows a map of Africa that identifies the 39 SSA countries that were eligible for AGOA benefits and the 10 SSA countries that were ineligible for AGOA benefits as of January 1, 2015.

Source: GAO analysis of Department of State and USAID data (data); Map Resources (map). | GAO-15-300.

Figure 1. Map of Sub-Saharan African Countries Eligible for African Growth and Opportunity Act (AGOA) Benefits, January 2015.

The U.S. Government Uses the Eligibility Review Process and the AGOA Forum to Engage with SSA Countries and Encourage Reforms

The U.S. government uses the annual eligibility review process and forum mandated by AGOA to engage with sub-Saharan African countries on their progress toward economic, political, and development reform objectives reflected in AGOA's eligibility criteria. USTR manages the annual consensus-based review process, which begins by collecting information from the public and other agencies of the AGOA Implementation Subcommittee. For SSA countries experiencing difficulty meeting one or more eligibility criteria, the U.S. government may decide on specific engagement actions to encourage reforms in specific areas. Over the lifetime of AGOA, 13 countries have lost their AGOA eligibility, although 7 countries eventually had their eligibility restored. The U.S. government uses the annual AGOA Forum to further engage with representatives from sub-Saharan Africa on challenges and encourage progress on AGOA's economic, political, and development reform objectives.

The AGOA Eligibility Review Is an Interagency Process Based on Consensus

The AGOA Implementation Subcommittee of the TPSC conducts the AGOA eligibility review annually to discuss whether a country has established or is making continual progress toward AGOA's reform objectives and makes consensus-based recommendations on each country's eligibility.[9] USTR's Office of African Affairs oversees the implementation of AGOA and chairs the AGOA Implementation Subcommittee. The full TPSC must review and approve the subcommittee's recommendations. The recommendations are then forwarded to the U.S. Trade Representative for review and approval. Once the recommendations are approved, the U.S. Trade Representative sends the recommendations to the President. The President makes the final decision on AGOA eligibility. The flow diagram in figure 2 provides an overview of the AGOA eligibility review process, organized into three phases: (1) initiation and data collection, (2) development of subcommittee recommendations, and (3) review and approval by the TPSC, USTR, and the President.

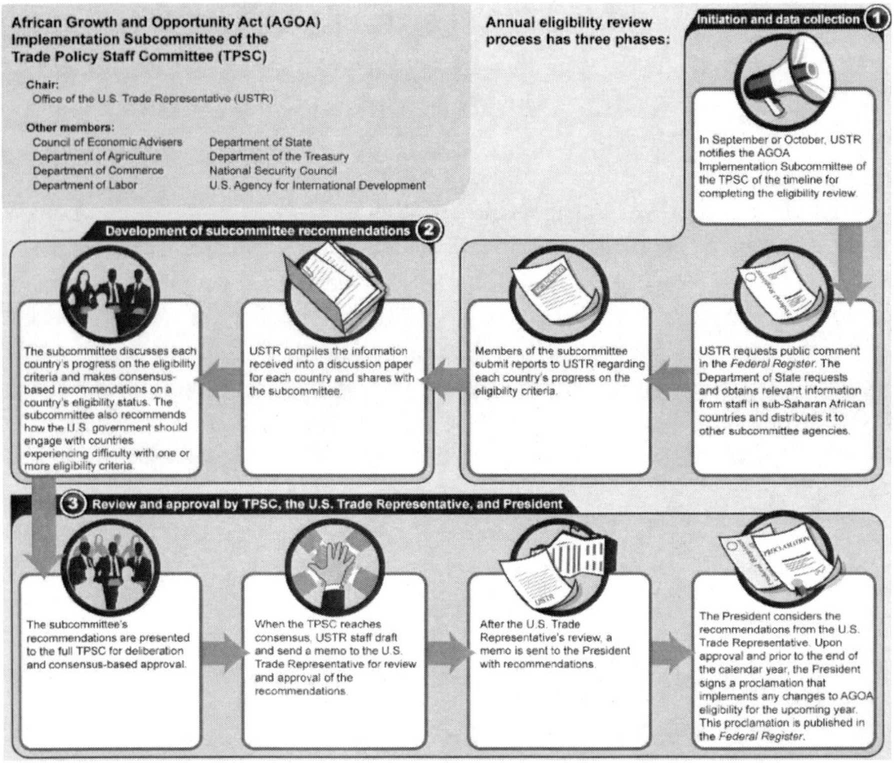

Source: GAO analysis of Office of the United States Trade Representative information. | GAO-15-300.

Figure 2. Overview of the African Growth and Opportunity Act (AGOA) Eligibility Review Process.

Phase 1: Initiation and Data Collection

Generally, USTR begins the annual eligibility review process in September or October by requesting that the agencies that form the AGOA Implementation Subcommittee— the Departments of Agriculture, Commerce, Labor, State, and the Treasury; USAID; Council of Economic Advisers; and National Security Council—provide information about each country's progress on reform objectives related to the eligibility criteria. USTR also requests public comments at this time. These agencies generally prepare and submit their reports to USTR by mid-October. State also distributes information collected by overseas staff on progress made by SSA countries on AGOA's reform objectives to the other members of the subcommittee to help inform the development of their reports. Subcommittee agencies frequently provide in-depth information related to the AGOA eligibility criteria that are most pertinent to their specific mission but may also provide input related to other eligibility criteria. For example, while the Department of Labor's reports primarily focus on labor issues, its reports on each country may also include information related to other eligibility criteria, such as human rights and the rule of law. (Table 2 identifies the primary focus of each subcommittee agency and the related AGOA reform objectives and corresponding eligibility criteria.)

Table 2. African Growth and Opportunity Act (AGOA) Implementation Subcommittee: Agencies, Primary Focus, and Related AGOA Reform Objectives and Corresponding Eligibility Criteria

Agency[a]	Primary focus[b]	Related AGOA reform objectives and corresponding eligibility criteria
Department of Agriculture	Food and agriculture and U.S. market access	**Economic** Market-based economy, elimination of barriers to U.S. trade and investment
Department of Commerce	Economic growth and development and trade promotion	**Economic** Market-based economy, elimination of barriers to U.S. trade and investment
Department of Labor	Labor issues	**Political** Protection of internationally recognized labor rights
Department of State	Economic growth and development, human rights, labor issues, corruption, foreign policy, and national security	**Economic and political** Rule of law, political pluralism, human rights, labor rights, and combating corruption
Department of the Treasury	Economic growth and development and global financial system	**Economic, political, and development** Market-based economy, rule of law, combatingcorruption, and poverty reduction
U.S. Agency for International Development	Broad-based economic growth and development through trade capacity building	**Development** Poverty reduction

Table 2. (Continued)

Agency[a]	Primary focus[b]	Related AGOA reform objectives and corresponding eligibility criteria
Office of the U.S. Trade Representative (USTR)	Trade and development, intellectual property, labor issues, and agriculture	**Economic, political, and development** Market-based economy, elimination of barriers to U.S. trade and investment, labor rights, and poverty reduction

Source: GAO analysis of Departments of Agriculture, Commerce, Labor, State, and the Treasury; U.S. Agency for International Development; and the Office of the U.S. Trade Representative information. | GAO-15-300.

[a]Traditionally, the Council of Economic Advisers and National Security Council have not provided reports to USTR on sub-Saharan African countries for the annual eligibility review. The Council on Economic Advisers covers issues related to international economic policy, and the National Security Council covers issues related to foreign policy and national security during the Implementation Subcommittee's discussion of each country's progress on the eligibility criteria.

[b]Subcommittee agencies frequently provide in-depth information related to the AGOA eligibility criteria that are most pertinent to their specific mission but may also provide input related to other eligibility criteria.

In phase 1 of the eligibility review process, USTR also publishes a notice in the *Federal Register* requesting public comment on SSA countries eligible to receive AGOA benefits. In 2013, USTR received 11 comments from a range of sources, including SSA governments, SSA private companies, a U.S. industry organization, a private U.S. citizen, a federation of U.S. unions, and a coalition of trade associations. The *Federal Register* notice and a presidential proclamation that finalizes eligibility decisions are the only components of the eligibility review process that are public.[10]

Phase 2: Development of Subcommittee Recommendations

USTR compiles the information provided by each subcommittee agency in phase 1 into a paper on each country. These papers also include broad-ranging information that USTR staff provide and any public comments that USTR receives in response to its notice in the *Federal Register.* USTR distributes the country papers to members of the AGOA Implementation Subcommittee for review and discussion at the subcommittee meeting. Typically, the AGOA Implementation Subcommittee convenes in November to review each country's progress in establishing or making continual progress toward AGOA's reform objectives. Usually, over a period that may range from a few days to a few weeks, the subcommittee works through each agency's priorities and viewpoints on each country's progress on the eligibility criteria, according to agency officials. The duration of this phase varies depending on how quickly the agencies can reach consensus. Any differences in perspective regarding countries' progress are discussed and consensus-based recommendations are reached.[11] For example, the U.S. Department of Agriculture has regularly raised concerns about progress on economic reform objectives in certain SSA countries, such as import bans and procedures to control pests and diseases in agricultural products. Countries have received démarches or letters for such issues; however, the subcommittee has not recommended that a SSA country lose its AGOA eligibility because of market access issues, according to USTR officials.[12]

Phase 3: Review and Approval by the TPSC, the U.S. Trade Representative, and the President

The subcommittee's recommendations are presented to the full TPSC for review and approval. After the TPSC reaches consensus, USTR staff prepare a decision memorandum for the U.S. Trade Representative's approval. The TPSC, the U.S. Trade Representative, and the President have the authority to modify the subcommittee's recommendations, according to agency officials. The U.S. Trade Representative prepares a decision memo with recommendations to the President for approval. Then, generally in December, the President issues a proclamation that implements any changes to SSA countries' AGOA eligibility status. The proclamation is published in the Federal Register.

Annual AGOA Eligibility Review Encourages U.S. Government Engagement with SSA Countries on Reforms

Regardless of a country's eligibility status, the U.S. government uses the eligibility review as one of many tools to initiate conversations with SSA countries about economic, political, and development reforms, according to agency officials. The subcommittee reviews each country individually, considering each country's particular situation, to determine how best to encourage progress toward specific eligibility criteria. The TPSC reviews the subcommittee's recommendations and makes the ultimate decision on specific actions the U.S. government can take to encourage countries to address particular concerns related to the eligibility criteria. For example, the TPSC may determine that the relevant U.S. ambassador, or other U.S. government official, should meet with appropriate country representatives. Other possible actions include issuing démarches or letters that describe the eligibility criteria concerns and outline actions the country may take to address those concerns. In some cases, the TPSC may recommend specific steps a country should take to maintain or restore its AGOA eligibility. After the TPSC's concerns are communicated to the country, relevant U.S. government officials manage engagement with the country and report back to the subcommittee on the country's progress. Although the eligibility review is annual, interim eligibility reviews may be held to gauge the progress countries are making on specific eligibility criteria. For example, in October 2011, an interim review reinstated AGOA eligibility for Côte d'Ivoire, Guinea, and Niger. All three countries had lost AGOA eligibility because of undemocratic changes in government and then regained eligibility following free and fair elections.

The following example illustrates how the U.S. government uses the eligibility review process to engage with SSA countries on issues related to specific reform objectives:

- **Swaziland** was deemed eligible for AGOA in January 2001. However, several years ago, the U.S. government began engaging with Swaziland on concerns related to internationally recognized labor rights through a series of letters and démarches issued by USTR and State. Over the course of several years, Swaziland made some progress on labor issues, but conditions related to labor rights later deteriorated. U.S. government officials met several times with Swaziland officials to discuss steps to improve labor rights, including a USTR-led interagency trip in April 2014. In particular, the officials were concerned that Swaziland had failed to make continual progress in protecting freedom of association and the right to organize. The U.S. officials were also concerned by Swaziland's use of security forces and arbitrary arrests to stifle peaceful demonstrations, and the lack of legal recognition for labor and employer federations. Despite U.S. efforts to engage with the country's government, Swaziland failed to make the necessary reforms. In June 2014, an interim review resulted in the President declaring Swaziland ineligible, effective as of January 1, 2015.

Since 2000, 13 Countries Have Lost Eligibility As a Result of Not Meeting Certain Eligibility Criteria; 7 Have Regained Eligibility

Over the lifetime of AGOA, 13 SSA countries have lost their AGOA eligibility for not meeting certain eligibility criteria, although 7 of these countries eventually had their AGOA eligibility restored. As of January 1, 2015, the 49 SSA countries fell into four categories based on their history of AGOA eligibility. (App. II provides a list of the SSA countries by eligibility status.)

- **Eligibility lost and regained.** Seven countries had lost AGOA eligibility at some time in the past but later regained it. Five of the countries experienced coups, one country lost eligibility after its President extended his term in violation of the country's constitution, and one country lost eligibility because of political unrest and armed conflict. All seven countries had their AGOA beneficiary status restored following a return to democratic rule. (Fig. 3 provides additional information regarding SSA countries that have lost and regained AGOA eligibility.)

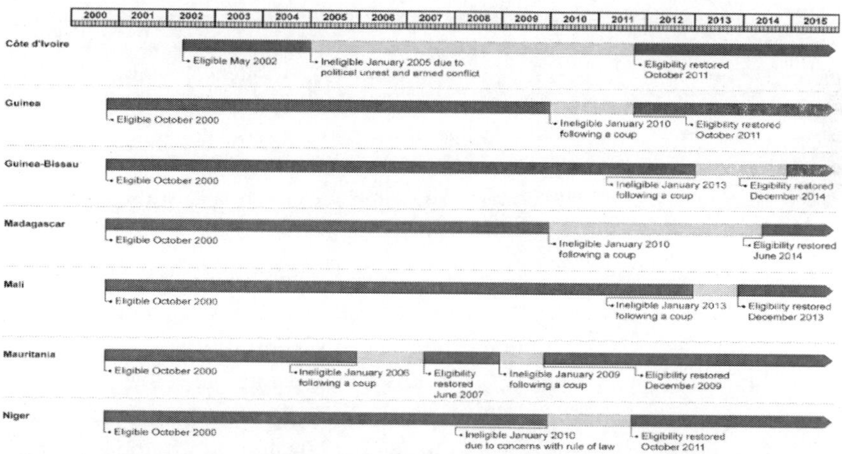

Source: GAO analysis of the Executive Office of the President, Department of State, the U.S. Agency for International Development, and the Office of the United States Trade Representative information. | GAO-15-300.

Figure 3. Timelines for Seven Sub-Saharan African Countries That Had Lost Eligibility for Benefits under the African Growth and Opportunity Act but Had Regained Eligibility before January 1, 2015.

- **Eligibility lost and not regained.** Six SSA countries have lost and not regained AGOA eligibility. One lost eligibility following a coup; three were deemed ineligible because of concerns about human rights abuses; one lost eligibility because of issues with labor rights; and one country lost eligibility following political violence and armed conflict. (Fig. 4 provides additional information regarding SSA countries that have lost and not regained AGOA eligibility.)

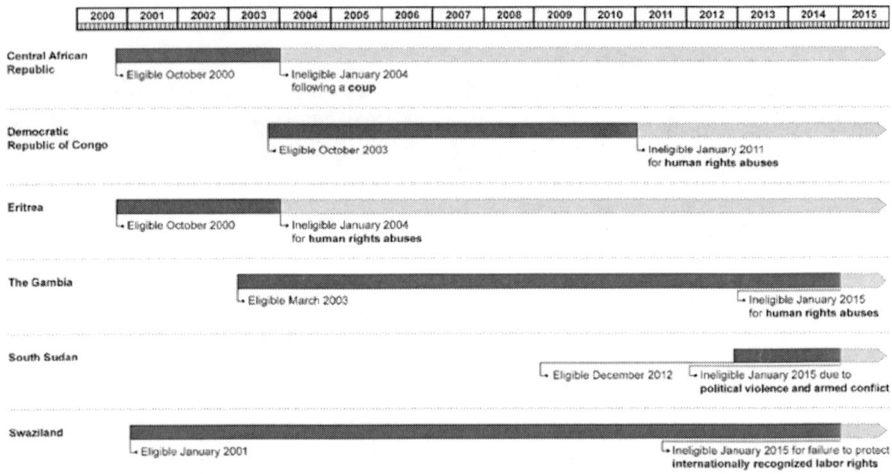

Source: GAO analysis of the Executive Office of the President, Department of State, the U.S. Agency for International Development, and the Office of the United States Trade Representative information. | GAO-15-300.

Figure 4. Timelines for Six Sub-Saharan African Countries That Lost Eligibility for Benefits under the African Growth and Opportunity Act and Had Not Regained Eligibility as of January 1, 2015.

- **Eligibility never lost.** About two-thirds of SSA countries, 32 of 49 countries have maintained their AGOA eligibility status since it was first granted. Six of 32 were not deemed eligible when AGOA was originally enacted in 2000. Although these countries had expressed interest in the AGOA trade preference program, they did not initially satisfy the eligibility criteria but later obtained eligibility for benefits under AGOA at different times.
- **Never eligible.** Four SSA countries have not been eligible for AGOA. Somalia and Sudan have not expressed official interest in the AGOA trade preference program, according to agency officials. Zimbabwe

and Equatorial Guinea have not been deemed eligible because of concerns related to AGOA's eligibility criteria.[13]

The AGOA Forum Promotes Trade and Investment Relations between the United States and Sub-Saharan Africa; Some Forum Activities Also Support AGOA Reform Objectives

The AGOA Forum is required under AGOA. Its purpose is to foster close economic ties between the United States and SSA countries; however, the forum also supports AGOA reform objectives by holding sessions that specifically address AGOA eligibility criteria.[14] The AGOA Forum is generally held in alternate years in the United States and sub-Saharan Africa and supports AGOA's reform objectives by facilitating high-level dialogue between the U.S. and SSA governments. The forum also engages the business community and civil society organizations. Generally, the forum takes place over 2 to 3 days and includes three to eight plenary sessions and several breakout sessions as well as workshops. Speakers are typically high-level U.S. and SSA government officials; however, speakers also include officials representing organizations such as the African Union and the United Nations Economic Commission for Africa. A number of U.S. congressional delegations have also participated in the forum. Civil society and private sector groups such as the Economic Justice Network and the African Cotton and Textile Industries Federation also actively participate in the forums.

The theme of the AGOA Forum changes from year to year, but the discussions are centered on strengthening the economic connection between the United States and sub-Saharan Africa. 15 For example, the theme of the December 2003 forum, hosted by the United States was "Building Trade, Expanding Investment" and the theme of the August 2013 forum, hosted by the Ethiopian government, was "Sustainable Transformation through Trade and Technology." The 2014 AGOA Forum consisted of a 1-day ministerial meeting that took place during the first U.S.-Africa Leaders Summit in Washington, D.C. This summit included leaders from SSA countries and other parts of Africa. (Table 3 provides the location and theme of each AGOA Forum from 2001 through 2014.)

Table 3. Location, Date, and Theme of African Growth and Opportunity Act (AGOA) Forums, 2001 to 2014

United States location and date	Theme	Sub-Saharan Africa location and date	Theme
Washington, D.C. (October 2001)	Enhancing Democracy and Combating HIV/AIDS	Port Luis, Mauritius (January 2003)	Trade and Investment: Tool for Growth and Development
Washington, D.C. (December 2003)	Building Trade, Expanding Investment	Dakar, Senegal (July 2005)	Expanding and Diversifying Trade toPromote Growth and Competitiveness
Washington, D.C. (June 2006)	Private Sector and Trade: Powering Africa's Growth	Accra, Ghana (July 2007)	As Trade Grows, Africa Prospers: Optimizing the Benefits under AGOA
Washington, D.C. (July 2008)	Mobilizing Private Investment for Trade and Growth	Nairobi, Kenya (August 2009)	Realizing the Full Potential of AGOAThrough Expansion of Trade and Investment
Washington, D.C. and Kansas City (August 2010)	AGOA at 10: New Strategies for a Changing World	Lusaka, Zambia (June 2011)	Enhanced Trade Through IncreasedCompetitiveness, Value Addition, and Deeper Regional Integration
Washington, D.C. (June 2012)	Enhancing Africa's Infrastructure for Trade	Addis Ababa, Ethiopia (August 2013)	Sustainable Transformation through Trade and Technology
Washington, D.C. (August 2014)	Investing in the Next Generation		

Source: GAO analysis of information from the Department of State and the Office of the United States Trade Representative. | GAO-15-300.

Although the annual AGOA Forums are trade-oriented, they also facilitate further engagement between the United States and SSA countries through dialogue about the reform objectives reflected in AGOA eligibility criteria. Throughout the years, AGOA Forum workshops have focused on a number of the eligibility criteria, including good governance, intellectual property rights, health care, and labor rights. For example, at the 2013 AGOA Forum in Addis Ababa, a session co-chaired by Liberian and U.S. senior government officials highlighted the importance of labor rights in achieving economic growth. As another example, breakout sessions at the 2009 and 2011 AGOA Forums focused on the relationship between good governance and the investment environment. During the forums, U.S. and SSA government officials also hold bilateral meetings to discuss specific issues related to AGOA's reform objectives and eligibility criteria, according to agency officials.

AGOA-Eligible Countries Have Fared Better than Ineligible Countries on Some Economic Development Indicators, but AGOA's Impact on Economic Development Is Difficult to Isolate

AGOA-eligible countries have fared better than ineligible countries on some economic development indicators since AGOA was enacted, according to our analysis of economic data for SSA countries that were eligible and ineligible for AGOA in 2012; however, AGOA's impact on economic development is difficult to isolate when additional factors are taken into consideration. Other factors—such as the small share of AGOA exports in the overall exports of many AGOA-eligible countries, the role of petroleum exports in recent income growth, the quality of government institutions, and different levels of foreign aid and investment—make it difficult to isolate how much economic development can be attributed to AGOA. For example, AGOA exports are a small share of overall exports for the majority of AGOA-eligible countries, a fact that could limit AGOA's impact on economic development in these countries. We found evidence that increasing energy prices may also have contributed to income growth within AGOA-eligible countries: from 2000 through 2012, the top three AGOA-eligible petroleum-exporting countries had a much higher growth rate for income per person than other AGOA-eligible countries. We also found that AGOA-eligible countries on average had higher governance scores and received more foreign aid and investment compared with ineligible countries. While these differences may have been facilitated by AGOA eligibility, they may also have contributed to economic development in AGOA-eligible countries, a possibility that makes it difficult to isolate AGOA's impact on economic development.

Since AGOA's Enactment, AGOA-Eligible Countries Have Had Higher Income per Person and Slightly Higher Growth Rates Compared with Ineligible Countries

Both before and since AGOA was enacted in 2000, income per person has been higher in AGOA-eligible countries, on average, compared with ineligible countries.[16] The average annual income per person for 37 AGOA-eligible countries was $876 in 2000, prior to AGOA's implementation, and $1,132 in 2012. The variation in income per person among the eligible countries was large; for example, in 2012, Seychelles had the highest income per person at $14,303 and Burundi had the lowest at $153. For 8 AGOA ineligible countries, average annual income per person was $353 in 2000 and $450 in 2012. Among the ineligible countries, income per person also varied widely. In 2012, Equatorial Guinea had the highest income per person at $14,199, whereas the Democratic Republic of Congo had the lowest at $165. The average annual growth in income per person was slightly higher in AGOA-eligible countries: eligible countries' income per person on average grew 2.2 percent per year from 2000 to 2012, compared with 2.1 percent per year in ineligible countries. Figure 5 shows trends in annual income per person from the enactment of AGOA through 2012, for eligible and ineligible countries. (For additional details on each country's annual income per person before and after AGOA, see app. III.)

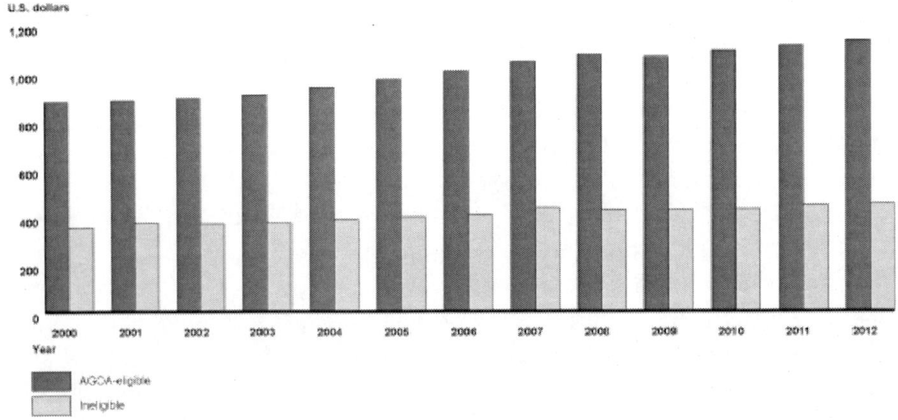

Source: GAO analysis of World Bank data. | GAO-15-300.

Figure 5. Annual Income per Person for African Growth and Opportunity Act (AGOA) Eligible Countries and Ineligible Countries, 2000-2012.

AGOA's Impact on Economic Development Is Difficult to Isolate after Additional Factors Are Considered

Exports under AGOA Accounted for a Small Proportion of Overall Exports for Most AGOA Countries

Exports under AGOA have accounted for a small proportion of exports for most AGOA-eligible countries. Our analysis shows that in 2013 AGOA exports accounted for less than 0.5 percent of overall exports for the majority of countries—for these countries, the small proportion of AGOA exports in their overall exports could limit AGOA's impact on economic development.[17] Figure 6 shows the number of AGOA-eligible countries in 2013 separated into categories based on the level of their exports under AGOA, as a share of their overall exports.[18]

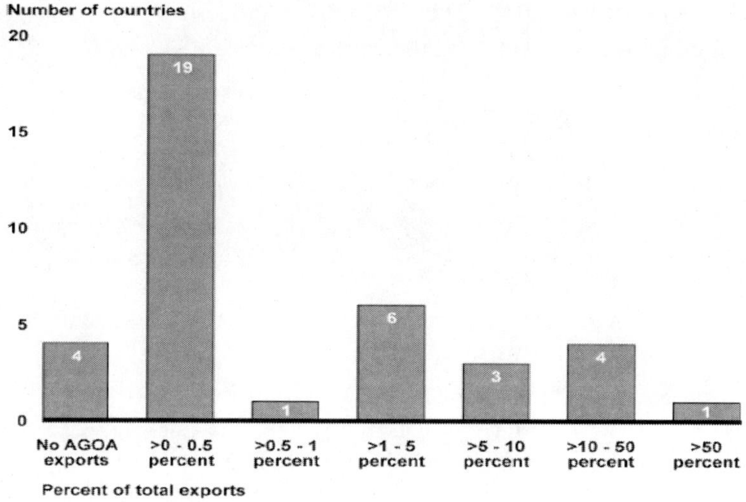

Source: GAO analysis of U.S. Census data. | GAO-15-300.

Note: We included exports claiming duty-free benefits under AGOA and the Generalized System of Preferences (GSP). The AGOA program provides duty-free access to products in addition to those products covered under GSP. AGOA countries continue to have duty-free access to the commodities covered under the GSP although that program expired in 2013. "AGOA-eligible countries" refers to sub-Saharan African countries eligible for AGOA benefits in 2013. Data were not available for South Sudan.

Figure 6. Exports under the African Growth and Opportunity Act (AGOA) as a Share of Total Exports for AGOA-Eligible Countries, 2013.

For example, 4 of the AGOA-eligible countries had no AGOA exports at all in 2013, and in the same year, AGOA accounted for less than 5 percent of overall exports for 26 other AGOA-eligible countries. In 2013, AGOA accounted for more than half of overall exports for only 1 country, Chad, a top petroleum exporter among AGOA-eligible countries.

Rising Energy Prices Affected Income Growth Rates of Top Petroleum Exporters among AGOA-Eligible Countries

While AGOA-eligible countries have had higher income per person than ineligible countries, the fastest growth in income per person has been concentrated in a few petroleum-exporting AGOA-eligible countries. From 2001 to 2013, petroleum products accounted for over 80 percent of U.S. imports under AGOA. Among AGOA-eligible countries, we identified Nigeria, Angola, and Chad as the top three petroleum exporting countries based on trade data in 2013. These countries collectively accounted for 90 percent of all petroleum exports to the United States under AGOA in 2013.

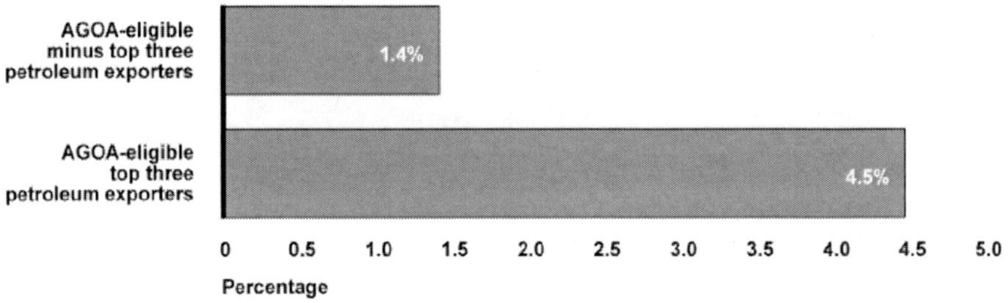

Source: GAO analysis of World Bank data. | GAO-15-300.

Notes: The chart shows average annual growth rate of population-weighted annual income per person from 2000 through 2012. "AGOA-eligible countries" refers to sub-Saharan African countries eligible for AGOA benefits in 2012. Averages were calculated for 37 AGOA-eligible countries that reported complete gross domestic product per capita data from 2000 through 2012: the top three petroleum exporting countries (Nigeria, Angola, and Chad), and 34 other AGOA-eligible countries. Djibouti, São Tomé and Principe, and South Sudan were excluded from the AGOA-eligible group because of missing data.

Figure 7. Annual Growth Rates in Income per Person, on Average, for African Growth and Opportunity Act (AGOA) Eligible Countries since AGOA's Implementation, Top Three Petroleum Exporters versus Other Eligible Countries, 2000-2012.

When we separated out these countries in our analysis, we found that from 2001 through 2012 the top three AGOA-eligible petroleum exporting countries as a group had, on average, slightly lower levels of annual income per person compared with all other AGOA-eligible countries considered as a group: $960 versus $1,026. However, figure 7 shows that from 2000 through 2012, these top three petroleum exporters had a much higher average annual growth rate as measured in income per person compared with the other AGOA-eligible countries: 4.5 percent per year versus 1.4 percent per year. The difference in income-perperson growth between the top three petroleum exporters and the other AGOA-eligible countries can be explained partly by rising energy prices.[19] From 2000 through 2012, global prices for petroleum increased by 272 percent.

AGOA-Eligible Countries Had Higher Governance Scores than Ineligible Countries Prior to AGOA

Prior to AGOA's implementation in 2000, the group of SSA countries eligible for AGOA benefits in 2012 had higher governance scores than ineligible countries. Academic studies have found a positive relationship between the quality of governance institutions and economic growth. Therefore, gains in economic growth since 2000 among AGOA-eligible countries may have been driven to some degree by governance that was more conducive to economic development. We analyzed two measures of institutional quality from the Worldwide Governance Indicators that capture some aspects of the security of private property, namely scores for the rule of law and political stability.[20] We found that AGOA-eligible countries had substantially higher scores on both rule of law and political stability in 2000 than countries that were not eligible for AGOA (see fig. 8). Pre-existing differences in institutional quality scores could explain in part why AGOA-eligible countries on average had higher annual income per person and slightly higher growth in annual income per person after the implementation of AGOA.

According to our analysis of the AGOA eligibility review process, given that governance is considered in the annual AGOA eligibility review, AGOA-eligible countries may also have benefited from an ongoing incentive to sustain or improve the quality of their governance institutions. Figure 8 shows that the differences in governance scores between eligible and ineligible countries in 2012 were similar to those in 2000. These persistent differences in the quality of governance institutions could also have contributed to the differences in economic growth between AGOA-eligible countries and ineligible countries after the implementation of AGOA.

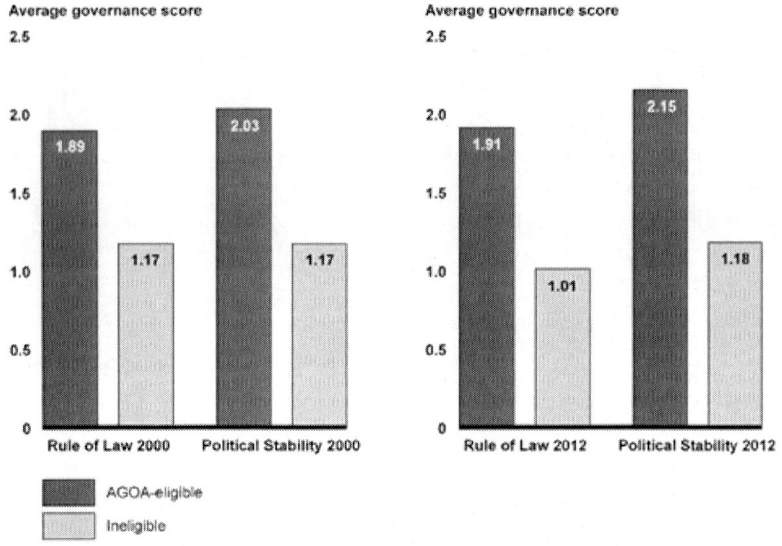

Source: GAO analysis of World Bank data. I GAO-15-300.

Notes: Governance scoring is on a scale of 0 to 5, with higher scores indicating better perceptions of governance. "AGOA-eligible countries" refers to sub-Saharan African countries that the U.S. government deemed eligible for AGOA benefits in 2012; "ineligible countries" refers to the other sub-Saharan African countries deemed ineligible for AGOA benefits in 2012.

Figure 8. Governance Scores for African Growth and Opportunity Act (AGOA) Eligible and Ineligible Countries, on Average, in 2000 and 2012.

AGOA-Eligible Countries Have Received More Foreign Aid and Investment than Ineligible Countries

AGOA-eligible countries on average have received more foreign aid per person and higher foreign direct investment (FDI) than ineligible countries since the implementation of AGOA.[21] The different levels of foreign aid and FDI, which could play a role in economic development and poverty reduction, also may have contributed to the differences in income per person between AGOA-eligible countries and ineligible countries that we observed.[22]

Moreover, according to our analysis of aid and investment flows to SSA countries (below), being eligible for AGOA may have improved the ability of countries to attract aid and investment.

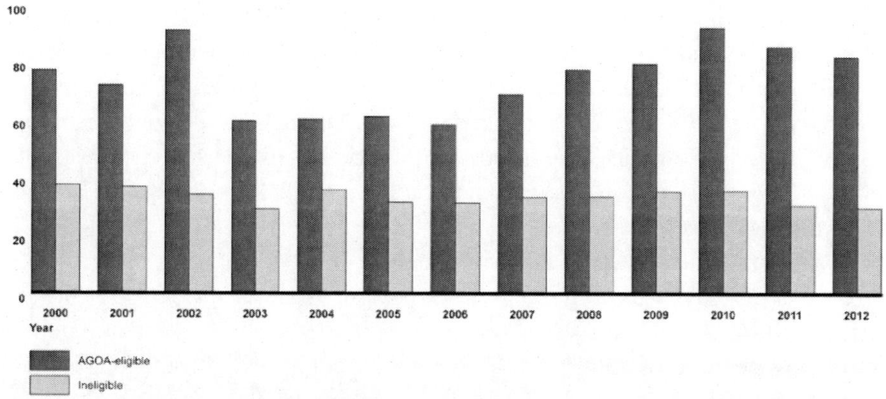

Source: GAO analysis of data from the Organisation for Economic Co-operation and Development and the World Bank. | GAO-15-300.

Notes: According to the Organisation for Economic Co-operation and Development, country programmable aid is the proportion of aid that is subjected to multiyear programming at the country level, and hence represents a subset of official development assistance flows. Amounts are in 2012 U.S. dollars. "AGOA-eligible countries" refers to sub-Saharan African countries that the U.S. government deemed eligible for AGOA benefits in 2012; "ineligible countries" refers to the other sub-Saharan African countries deemed ineligible for AGOA benefits in 2012.

Figure 9. Country Programmable Aid Received per Person for African Growth and Opportunity Act (AGOA) Eligible and Ineligible Countries, on Average, 2000-2012.

Our analysis shows that on average AGOA-eligible countries received more foreign aid per person than ineligible countries. We analyzed data on country programmable aid (CPA) from the Organisation for Economic Co-operation and Development (OECD). According to the OECD, CPA captures the main cross-border aid flows to recipient countries and excludes some forms of official development assistance that are neither fully transparent to, nor manageable by, recipient countries, including humanitarian aid in response to crises and natural disasters, and debt relief provided by donor nations. The United States allocated an estimated $7.04 billion in U.S. bilateral aid to Africa in fiscal year 2014. The aid was intended to help SSA countries in areas including health; climate change; food security; and, more recently, power.

From 2000 to 2012, AGOA-eligible countries received more than twice as much aid per person on average than ineligible countries (see fig. 9).

AGOA-eligible countries on average also received more FDI than ineligible countries. According to a 2014 U.S. International Trade Commission report, global inflows from FDI into SSA countries increased almost sixfold between 2000 and 2012.[23] We analyzed FDI as a share of a country's gross domestic product (GDP) to take into consideration the size of the country's economy. From 2001 to 2013, the amount of FDI each SSA country received relative to the size of its overall economy varied considerably. For example, among SSA countries that were net recipients of FDI in 2013, Burundi received FDI amounting to less than half a percent of its GDP (the lowest in sub-Saharan Africa), while Liberia received FDI amounting to about 57 percent of its GDP (the highest in sub-Saharan Africa). From 2001 through 2013, AGOA-eligible countries received FDI that on average amounted to about 5.6 percent of GDP, while ineligible countries averaged about 2.7 percent. (See fig. 10.)

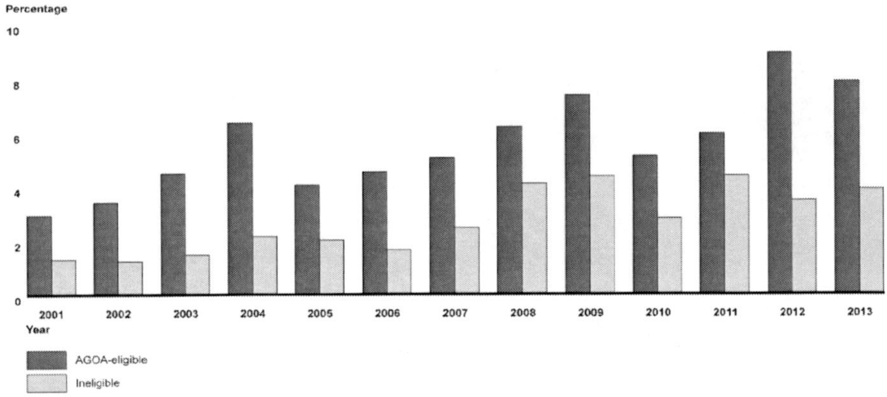

Source: GAO analysis of World Bank World Development Indicators data. | GAO-15-300.

Note: We did not include Equatorial Guinea in the AGOA-ineligible group because the foreign direct investment data for 2002 were deemed unreliable. "AGOA-eligible countries" refers to sub-Saharan African countries that the U.S. government deemed eligible for AGOA benefits in 2012; "ineligible countries" refers to the other sub-Saharan African countries deemed ineligible for AGOA benefits in 2012.

Figure 10. Foreign Direct Investment as a Percentage of Gross Domestic Product, on Average, in African Growth and Opportunity Act (AGOA) Eligible and Ineligible Countries, 2001-2013.

Being eligible for AGOA may help a country attract aid and investment. For example, AGOA eligibility can be seen as a signal of a relatively stable political environment as well as advantages in tariff treatment for certain products. According to a recent report by the U.S. International Trade Commission, AGOA has signaled improvements in the business and investment climate in SSA countries, and has contributed to increasing FDI flows to these countries.[24] Additionally, the International Monetary Fund reported in June 2014 that in Swaziland uncertain prospects for AGOA eligibility could affect investment and employment in the textile sector.[25] Similarly, Ethiopian government officials in the Ministry of Trade said that AGOA has helped to attract foreign direct investment to Ethiopia.

AGOA's Impact on Economic Development Is Difficult to Isolate

Our analysis of factors contributing to economic development in SSA countries and review of academic literature suggest that isolating AGOA's impact on overall economic development is difficult. We found that on average, AGOA-eligible countries have had higher annual income per person and slightly higher growth rates in annual income per person than ineligible countries; we also found evidence suggesting that AGOA eligibility might be associated with other factors that also can positively affect development. For example, our review of academic literature indicated that increased FDI could enhance countries' economic growth, and our analysis demonstrated that on average AGOA-eligible countries receive more FDI inflows relative to the size of their economies.

Agency Comments

We are not making any recommendations in this report. We provided a draft of this report for comment to the Departments of Agriculture, Commerce, Labor, State, and the Treasury; USAID; and the Office of the U.S. Trade Representative (USTR). The Departments of Labor, State, the Treasury, and USTR provided technical comments, which we have incorporated in the report, as appropriate.

Thomas Melito
Director, International Affairs and Trade

APPENDIX I: OBJECTIVES, SCOPE, AND METHODOLOGY

Our objectives were to examine (1) how the African Growth and Opportunity Act (AGOA) eligibility review process has considered and the AGOA Forums have supported economic, political, and development reform objectives described in the act and (2) how sub-Saharan African (SSA) countries have fared in certain economic development outcomes since the enactment of AGOA.

To examine how the U.S. government's process for determining AGOA eligibility and the AGOA Forums have supported reform objectives established in sections 104 and 105 of the act, we reviewed the AGOA legislation and documents from the seven U.S. agencies relevant to the AGOA eligibility criteria. We analyzed the AGOA eligibility status of SSA countries and the implementation of AGOA Forum activities since AGOA's original enactment to identify changes in eligibility from 2000 through January 2015. We also attended and observed 2014 AGOA Forum events.

To address both objectives, we interviewed officials from the Departments of Agriculture, Commerce, Labor, State, and the Treasury; the U.S. Agency for International Development; and the Office of the U.S. Trade Representative (USTR), all of which are the members of the Trade Policy Staff Committee's AGOA Implementation Subcommittee that generally prepare the sub-Saharan Africa country reports for the annual eligibility review.[1]

To examine the relationship between AGOA eligibility and economic development in sub-Saharan Africa, we analyzed data on gross domestic product (GDP) per capita and total population from the World Bank World Development Indicators. We used data from the April 2014 version of the World Development Indicators. We compared population-weighted average GDP per capita at the end of 2012 for AGOA-eligible countries versus ineligible countries, as well as for the top three AGOA-eligible petroleum exporting countries versus other AGOA-eligible countries. We also compared average annual growth rates in annual income per person from 2000 to 2012 for AGOA-eligible versus ineligible countries, as well as for the top three AGOA-eligible petroleum exporting countries versus other AGOA-eligible countries. To study sub-Saharan African countries' exports under AGOA as a share of total exports as well as the value of petroleum exports to the United States under AGOA, we used U.S. Census trade data on imports by trading partners and imports by product from 2013. We used data on countries' total exports from the International Monetary Fund's Direction of Trade Statistics and International Financial Statistics databases. We calculated AGOA-eligible countries' shares of AGOA and Generalized System of Preference (GSP) exports in their overall exports to study how the value of exports under these trade preference systems compared with the value of overall exports for AGOAeligible countries in 2013. To study differences in the quality of governance institutions between AGOA-eligible and ineligible countries, we analyzed data on governance from the World Bank Worldwide Governance Indicators, comparing average scores for Political Stability and Rule of Law in 2000 and 2012 between AGOA-eligible and ineligible countries. To describe the differences in the amount of foreign development assistance and foreign direct investment received by AGOA-eligible and ineligible countries, we used data on country programmable aid from the Organisation for Economic Co-operation and Development (OECD) and foreign direct investment (FDI) as a percentage of GDP from the World Development Indicators. We compared yearly averages of aid per capita (from 2000 to 2012) and net FDI inflows as a percentage of GDP (from 2001 to 2013) between AGOAeligible and ineligible countries. To assess the reliability of these data, we reviewed publicly available documents on these databases and conducted electronic testing for missing values and outliers. We determined that the data were sufficiently reliable for our purposes. We also reviewed a judgmental sample of peer-reviewed academic literature related to economic development, foreign direct investment, foreign aid, and the impact of trade preference programs.

Country classifications. For most of the analysis, we defined AGOA-eligible countries as the 40 SSA countries that were deemed eligible for AGOA benefits as of the end of 2012. Nine SSA countries were ineligible for AGOA benefits as of the end of 2012. We chose 2012 as the base year for this classification because it was the latest year for which data on GDP per capita were available for the SSA countries in the April 2014 version of the World Bank World Development Indicators. The only exception is that for the analysis of the exports under AGOA as a share of total exports from AGOA-eligible countries, we defined AGOA-eligible countries as the 39 countries that were deemed eligible for AGOA benefits as of 2013 because we analyzed 2013 trade statistics.

GDP per capita. To study differences and depict trends in income per person between selected groupings of countries, we used the World Development Indicators annual GDP per capita series, expressed in year 2005 U.S. dollars. Thirty-seven out of 40 countries eligible for AGOA benefits in 2012, and 8 out of 9 ineligible countries, reported complete GDP per capita data from 2000 and through 2012. Djibouti, São Tomé and Principe, and South

Sudan were excluded from the AGOA-eligible group because of missing data. Somalia was excluded from the ineligible group due to missing data. Within each country grouping, we took the weighted average of countries' GDP per capita, where the weights are given by the share of a country's population in the overall group's population. The weighted average GDP per capita is a measure of the yearly income of the average individual in the country group. Equation (1) shows that the weighted average GDP per capita is equivalent to summing up the GDP of every country in the group and dividing by the total group population:

$$\sum_{i=1}^{n} \frac{y_i}{L_i} \times \frac{L_i}{\sum_{j=1}^{n} L_j} = \frac{\sum_{i=1}^{n} y_i}{\sum_{j=1}^{n} L_j} \tag{1}$$

Where n denotes the number of countries in the group, yi refers to gross domestic product of country i, and Li refers to the population of country i.

AGOA export share. To examine the magnitude of AGOA exports relative to the total exports of each AGOA-eligible country, we used U.S. Census data on imports by trading partners. We calculated the value of imports under AGOA (i.e., imports that received duty-free access claiming AGOA preference benefits) and imports that received duty-free access under GSP. Since AGOA was established as a program for SSA countries that builds on GSP, we analyzed exports from AGOA-eligible countries to the United States under both programs together. AGOA countries continue to have duty-free access to the commodities covered under the GSP although that program expired in 2013. We computed the AGOA (including GSP) share of exports relative to total exports for each AGOA-eligible country in 2013, and graphically tabulated countries according to their AGOA export share. In this analysis, both the exports data and the definition of AGOA eligibility are from 2013. We used data from two International Monetary Fund databases, Direction of Trade and International Financial Statistics, to determine total exports for each country.

Top three AGOA-eligible petroleum exporters. The top three AGOA-eligible petroleum exporters were Nigeria, Angola, and Chad, which collectively accounted for 90 percent of all petroleum exports to the U.S. under AGOA in 2013, based on U.S. Census data on AGOA imports by product. Since AGOA was established as a program for SSA countries that builds on GSP, the 90 percent statistic refers to exports of petroleum from

AGOA-eligible countries to the United States under both programs together. AGOA countries continue to have duty-free access to the commodities covered under the GSP although that program expired in 2013. AGOA-eligible countries minus the top petroleum exporters refer to the remaining 34 AGOA-eligible countries.

Governance. To examine differences in the quality of governance (also known as "institutions") between AGOA-eligible and ineligible countries, we reviewed a judgmental sample of empirical academic literature that provided evidence that property rights and political stability can promote economic growth.[2] We judgmentally identified two measures of institutional quality from the Worldwide Governance Indicators that may capture aspects of the security of private property, namely scores for the rule of law and political stability. We compared the simple average of scores in 2000 and 2012 for AGOA-eligible countries versus ineligible countries. We rescaled the indicators to range from 0 to 5, with higher scores indicating better perceptions of governance.

Aid and foreign direct investment. To examine differences in the amount of development assistance received by AGOA-eligible versus ineligible countries, we used annual data from the OECD on country programmable aid. According to the OECD, country programmable aid (CPA) is the proportion of aid that is subjected to multiyear programming at the country level, and hence represents a subset of official development assistance (ODA) flows. CPA is equivalent to gross ODA disbursements by recipient but excludes spending that is (1) inherently unpredictable (humanitarian aid and debt relief); or (2) entails no flows to the recipient country (administration costs, student costs, development awareness and research, and refugee spending in donor countries); or (3) is usually not discussed between the main donor agency and recipient governments (food aid, aid from local governments, core funding to nongovernmental organizations, aid through secondary agencies, ODA equity investments, and aid that is not allocable by country). CPA counts loan repayments among the aid transferred from donor countries to developing countries. We represented country programmable aid in per person units by dividing the program aid total by the total population of the country. Data on population were from the World Development Indicators. We computed the simple average of aid per person in each year from 2005 to 2012 for AGOA-eligible countries and AGOA ineligible countries.

To examine differences in the amount of foreign direct investment received by AGOA-eligible versus ineligible countries, we used annual data on net inflows of foreign direct investment as a percentage of GDP from the

World Bank World Development Indicators. We computed the simple average of these series in each year from 2001 to 2013 for AGOAeligible countries and AGOA ineligible countries. In using the FDI data, we checked for outliers and missing values and identified Equatorial Guinea as an outlier based on comparisons with data from other sources; values for Equatorial Guinea's net FDI inflows as a percentage of GDP were omitted from the calculation of the average.

We conducted this performance audit from April 2014 to February 2015 in accordance with generally accepted government auditing standards. Those standards require that we plan and perform the audit to obtain sufficient, appropriate evidence to provide a reasonable basis for our findings and conclusions based on our audit objectives. We believe that the evidence obtained provides a reasonable basis for our findings and conclusions based on our audit objectives.

APPENDIX II: AFRICAN GROWTH AND OPPORTUNITY ACT (AGOA) ELIGIBILITY STATUS FOR SUB-SAHARAN COUNTRIES AS OF JANUARY 2015

Sub-Saharan countries	Eligibility lost and regained	Eligibility lost and not regained	Eligibility never lost	Never eligible
Angola (eligible Dec. 30, 2003)			√	
Benin (eligible Oct. 2, 2000)			√	
Botswana (eligible Oct. 2, 2000)			√	
Burkina Faso (eligible Dec. 10, 2004)			√	
Burundi (eligible Dec. 22, 2005)			√	
Cameroon (eligible Oct. 2, 2000)			√	
Cape Verde (eligible Oct. 2, 2000)			√	
Central African Republic (eligible Oct. 2, 2000; ineligible Jan. 1, 2004)		√		
Chad (eligible Oct. 2, 2000)			√	

Sub-Saharan countries	Eligibility lost and regained	Eligibility lost and not regained	Eligibility never lost	Never eligible
Comoros (eligible June 30, 2008)			√	
Congo, Democratic Republic of(eligible Oct. 31, 2003; ineligible Jan. 1, 2011)		√		
Congo, Republic of (eligible Oct. 2, 2000)			√	
Côted'Ivoire (eligible May 16, 2002; ineligible Jan. 1, 2005; eligibility regained Oct. 25, 2011)	√			
Djibouti (eligible Oct. 2, 2000)			√	
Equatorial Guinea				√
Eritrea (eligible Oct. 2, 2000; ineligible Jan. 1, 2004)		√		
Ethiopia (eligible Oct. 2, 2000)			√	
Gabon (eligible Oct. 2, 2000)			√	
Gambia, The (eligible Mar. 28, 2003; Ineligible Jan. 1, 2015)		√		
Ghana (eligible Oct. 2, 2000)			√	
Guinea (eligible Oct. 2, 2000; ineligible Jan. 1, 2010; eligibility regained Oct. 25, 2011)	√			
Guinea-Bissau (eligible Oct. 2, 2000; ineligible Jan. 1, 2013; Eligible Dec. 23, 2014)	√			
Kenya (eligible Oct. 2, 2000)			√	
Lesotho (eligible Oct. 2, 2000)			√	
Liberia (eligible Dec. 29, 2006)			√	
Madagascar (eligible Oct. 2, 2000; ineligible Jan. 1, 2010; eligibility regained June 26, 2014)	√			
Malawi (eligible Oct. 2, 2000)			√	
Mali (eligible Oct. 2, 2000; ineligible Jan. 1, 2013; eligibility regained Dec. 23, 2013)	√			

Appendix II. (Continued)

Sub-Saharan countries	Eligibility lost and regained	Eligibility lost and not regained	Eligibility never lost	Never eligible
Mauritania (eligible Oct. 2, 2000; ineligible Jan.1, 2006; eligibility regained June 28, 2007; ineligible Jan. 2009; eligibility regained Dec. 23,2009)	√			
Mauritius (eligible Oct. 2, 2000)			√	
Mozambique (eligible Oct. 2, 2000)			√	
Namibia (eligible Oct. 2, 2000)			√	
Niger (eligible October 2, 2000; ineligible Jan. 1, 2010; eligibility regained Oct. 25, 2011)	√			
Nigeria (eligible Oct. 2, 2000)			√	
Rwanda (eligible Oct. 2, 2000)			√	
São Tomé and Principe (eligible Oct. 2, 2000)			√	
Senegal (eligible Oct. 2, 2000)			√	
Seychelles (eligible Oct. 2, 2000)			√	
Sierra Leone (eligible Oct. 2, 2000)			√	
Somalia				√
South Africa (eligible Oct. 2, 2000)			√	
South Sudan (eligible Dec. 20, 2012; ineligible Jan. 1, 2015)		√		
Sudan				√
Swaziland (eligible Jan. 17, 2001; ineligible Jan. 1, 2015)		√		
Tanzania (eligible Oct. 2, 2000)			√	
Togo (eligible Apr. 17, 2008)			√	
Uganda (eligible Oct. 2, 2000)			√	
Zambia (eligible Oct. 2, 2000)			√	
Zimbabwe				√

Source: GAO analysis of presidential proclamations. | GAO-15-300

APPENDIX III: ANNUAL INCOME PER PERSON (GDP PER CAPITA) IN SUB-SAHARAN AFRICAN COUNTRIES IN 2000 AND 2012 AND AGOA ELIGIBILITY STATUS IN 2012

Inflation-adjusted U.S. dollars (2005 base year)			
Country	**GDP per capita in 2000**	**GDP per capita in 2012**	**AGOA-eligible in 2012**
Angola	1,238	2,686	Yes
Benin	513	568	Yes
Botswana	4,736	6,684	Yes
Burkina Faso	343	493	Yes
Burundi	150	153	Yes
Cameroon	868	964	Yes
Cape Verde	1,866	3,321	Yes
Central African Republic	339	472	No
Chad	367	738	Yes
Comoros	639	606	Yes
Côte d'Ivoire	1,014	958	Yes
Congo, Democratic Republic of	124	165	No
Congo, Republic of	1,596	1,944	Yes
Djibouti	847	No data available	Yes
Equatorial Guinea	4,708	14,199	No
Eritrea	246	200	No
Ethiopia	135	253	Yes
Gabon	6,488	6,709	Yes
Gambia, The	438	441	Yes
Ghana	446	724	Yes
Guinea	289	308	Yes
Guinea-Bissau	416	397	No
Kenya	501	595	Yes
Lesotho	640	929	Yes
Liberia	167	276	Yes
Madagascar	286	273	No
Malawi	221	220	Yes
Mali	380	480	Yes
Mauritania	643	835	Yes
Mauritius	4,555	6,496	Yes
Mozambique	236	417	Yes

Appendix III. (Continued)

Inflation-adjusted U.S. dollars (2005 base year)			
Country	**GDP per capita in 2000**	**GDP per capita in 2012**	**AGOA-eligible in 2012**
Namibia	3,007	4,373	Yes
Niger	255	290	Yes
Nigeria	679	1,053	Yes
Rwanda	211	390	Yes
São Tomé and Principe	No data available	840	Yes
Senegal	703	797	Yes
Seychelles	11,492	14,303	Yes
Sierra Leone	276	435	Yes
Somalia	No data available	No data available	No
South Africa	4,652	5879	Yes
South Sudan	No data available	No data available	Yes
Sudan	566	837	No
Swaziland	2,189	2341	Yes
Tanzania	304	483	Yes
Togo	411	413	Yes
Uganda	268	405	Yes
Zambia	562	798	Yes
Zimbabwe	676	431	No

Source: GAO analysis of World Bank data. | GAO-15-300.

Note: Data are from the April 2014 version of the World Development Indicators.

End Notes

[1] AGOA was originally enacted as Pub. L. No. 106-200, May 18, 2000. Since its enactment, AGOA has been amended three times, by Pub. L. No. 107-210, August 6, 2002; Pub. L. No. 108-274, July 12, 2004; and Pub. L. No. 109-432, December 20, 2006.

[2] We have previously issued the following related reports: GAO, *African Growth and Opportunity Act: Observations on Competitiveness and Diversification of U.S. Imports from Beneficiary Countries*, GAO-14-722R (Washington, D.C.: July 21, 2014), and *African Growth and Opportunity Act: USAID Could Enhance Utilization by Working with More Countries to Develop Export Strategies,* GAO-15-218 (Washington, D.C.: Jan. 22, 2015).

[3] The AGOA Implementation Subcommittee of the TPSC consists of nine agencies, seven of which have generally provided country reports for the annual eligibility review meeting.

The Council of Economic Advisers and the National Security Council, which also serve on the subcommittee, generally have not provided country reports.

[4] The 40 AGOA-eligible countries as of the end of 2012 were Angola, Benin, Botswana, Burkina Faso, Burundi, Cameroon, Cape Verde, Chad, Comoros, Republic of Congo, Côte d'Ivoire, Djibouti, Ethiopia, Gabon, The Gambia, Ghana, Guinea, Kenya, Lesotho, Liberia, Malawi, Mali, Mauritania, Mauritius, Mozambique, Namibia, Niger, Nigeria, Rwanda, São Tomé and Principe, Senegal, Seychelles, Sierra Leone, South Africa, South Sudan, Swaziland, Tanzania, Togo, Uganda, and Zambia. The 9 AGOA-ineligible countries in 2012 were Central African Republic, Democratic Republic of Congo, Equatorial Guinea, Eritrea, Guinea-Bissau, Madagascar, Somalia, Sudan, and Zimbabwe.

[5] Pub. L. No. 106-200, May 18, 2000, section 104(a)(1).

[6] The United States offered tariff reductions for goods from most sub-Saharan African countries under the Generalized System of Preferences, a preferential tariff system for designated beneficiary developing countries. The Africa Investment Incentive Act of 2006, Pub. L. No. 109-432, div. D, Title VI, expanded the list of products that eligible sub-Saharan African countries may export to the United States duty-free under GSP, which covers approximately 4,600 items. Although legal authorization of the GSP program expired on July 31, 2013, imports of GSP-eligible imports from AGOA countries will continue to be eligible for duty-free entry, pursuant to the provisions of the statute governing the AGOA program.

[7] Office of the U.S. Trade Representative and the U.S. Agency for International Development, *African Growth and Opportunity Act Implementation Guide* (Washington, D.C.: October 2000).

[8] The two SSA countries that have never requested AGOA benefits are Somalia and Sudan, according to USTR officials.

[9] The TPSC is a U.S. interagency mechanism for trade policy coordination. USTR chairs the TPSC, which consists of USTR and 20 other U.S. government entities. TPSC members include the Office of the U.S. Trade Representative (chair), Council of Economic Advisers, Council of Environmental Quality, Department of Agriculture, Department of Commerce, Department of Defense, Department of Energy, Department of Health and Human Services, Department of Homeland Security, Department of the Interior, Department of Justice, Department of Labor, Department of State, Department of Transportation, Department of the Treasury, Environmental Protection Agency, U.S. Agency for International Development, National Economic Council, National Security Council, Office of Management and Budget, and the United States International Trade Commission (nonvoting member).

[10] From 2001 through 2008, AGOA required USTR to report on the implementation of AGOA. The reports included a summary of the outcomes of the annual eligibility review and an evaluation of each country's strengths and weaknesses in relation to each of the eligibility criteria. Congress did not renew the reporting requirement after its sunset date.

[11] Occasionally, when the subcommittee is unable to reach consensus, the TPSC may have to deliberate and reach consensus on particular countries' eligibility in phase 3, according to agency officials

[12] A démarche is a formal diplomatic representation of one government's official position, views, or wishes on a given subject to an appropriate official in another government or international organization. Démarches generally seek to persuade, inform, or gather information from a foreign government.

[13] Effective in 2011 Equatorial Guinea was no longer considered for AGOA benefits because it was determined to be high-income and became ineligible for GSP. AGOA requires that SSA countries be eligible for GSP in order to be considered for AGOA.

[14] AGOA also requires the President to instruct the U.S. delegates to the forum to promote a review by the forum of the HIV/AIDS epidemic in each SSA country and the effect of the HIV/AIDS epidemic on each country's economic development.

[15] The costs of U.S.-hosted AGOA Forums are shared by U.S. agencies, according to U.S. State Department officials. When the forum is held in Africa, the host government bears the cost of hosting the event, including the cost of the venue, conference services, security, and transportation.

[16] For this analysis, we used data on gross domestic product (GDP) per capita (measured in 2005 U.S. dollars) and total population from the World Bank World Development Indicators. Thirty-seven out of 40 countries eligible for AGOA benefits in 2012, and 8 out of 9 ineligible countries, reported complete GDP per capita data from 2000 through 2012. Djibouti, São Tomé and Principe, and South Sudan were excluded from the set of AGOA-eligible countries we analyzed because of missing data. Somalia was excluded from the set of ineligible countries we analyzed because of missing data.

[17] For this analysis of year 2013 export data, we refer to the set of "AGOA-eligible countries" as the 39 countries eligible for AGOA benefits in 2013. The only difference relative to the list of AGOA-eligible countries in 2012 is that Mali was removed from the list of AGOA-eligible countries in 2013.

[18] We report both AGOA and Generalized System of Preferences (GSP) exports in fig. 6 (and related text below on petroleum exports) because the AGOA program provides duty-free access to products in addition to those products covered under GSP. AGOA countries continue to have duty-free access to the commodities covered under the GSP, although that program expired in 2013. Including GSP exports in the figure gives a conservative— that is, a higher value—estimate of the level of a country's AGOA exports as a share of its overall exports.

[19] AGOA trade preferences provide tariff benefits to petroleum exports from AGOA countries. However, the tariff margin is relatively small, ranging from 5 cents to 10 cents per barrel. Academic studies measuring the impact of AGOA have found that AGOA has had little to no direct impact on petroleum exports. See, for example, B. Seyoum, "Export Performance of Developing Countries under the African Growth and Opportunity Act," *Journal of Economic Studies*, vol. 34, no. 6 (2007); N. Condon and M. Stern, "The Effectiveness of African Growth and Opportunity Act in Increasing Trade from Least Developed Countries: A Systematic Review," EPPI-Centre, Social Science Research Unit, Institute of Education, University of London (2010); and G. Frazer and J. Van Biesebroeck, "Trade Growth under the African Growth and Opportunity Act," *Review of Economics and Statistics,* vol. 90, no. 1 (2010).

[20] Worldwide Governance Indicator scores are composites of a large number of surveys of enterprises, citizens, and experts gathered from a number of survey institutes, think tanks, nongovernmental organizations, international organizations, and private sector firms. Rule of law is defined as perceptions of the extent to which agents have confidence in and abide by the rules of society, and in particular the quality of contract enforcement, property rights, the police, and the courts, as well as the likelihood of crime and violence. Political stability is defined as perceptions of the likelihood that the government will be destabilized or overthrown by unconstitutional or violent means, including politically-motivated violence

and terrorism. See World Bank Worldwide Governance Indicators at http://info.worldbank.org/governance/wgi/index.aspx#home.

[21] According to the World Bank, foreign direct investment is investment in an enterprise that operates outside the investor's country, which establishes a lasting interest in or effective management control over an enterprise. Foreign direct investment can include buying shares of an enterprise in another country, reinvesting earnings of a foreign-owned enterprise in the country where it is located, and parent firms extending loans to their foreign affiliates.

[22] The economics literature has long recognized the benefits of FDI on economic development. See for example L. Alfaro, A. Chanda, S. Kalemli-Ozcan, and S. Sayek, "FDI and Economic Growth: The Role of Local Financial Markets," *Journal of International Economics*, vol. 64, no. 1 (2004); and U. Nair-Reichert and D. Weinhold, "Causality Tests for Cross-Country Panels: a New Look at FDI and Economic Growth in Developing Countries," *Oxford Bulletin of Economics and Statistics*, vol. 63, no. 2 (2001).

[23] U.S. International Trade Commission, *AGOA: Trade and Investment Performance Overview*, Pub. No.: 4461 (Washington, D.C.: April 2014).

[24] U.S. International Trade Commission, *AGOA: Trade and Investment Performance Overview*, Pub. No.: 4461 (Washington, D.C: April 2014).

[25] International Monetary Fund, *Kingdom of Swaziland: 2014 Article IV Consultation—Staff Report; and Press Release*, IMF Country Report No. 14/223 (Washington, D.C: July 2014).

End Notes for Appendix I

[1] The AGOA Implementation Subcommittee of the Trade Policy Staff Committee (TPSC) consists of 9 agencies, of which 7 have generally provided country reports for the annual eligibility review meeting. The Council of Economic Advisers and the National Security Council generally have not provided country reports to date. The TPSC is a U.S. interagency mechanism for trade policy coordination. USTR chairs the TPSC, which consists of USTR and 20 other U.S. government entities.

[2] D. Acemoglu, S. Johnson, and J.A. Robinson, "The Colonial Origins of Comparative Development: An Empirical Investigation," *American Economic Review*, vol. 91, no.5 (2001); D. Rodrik, A. Subramanian, and F. Trebbi, "Institutions Rule: The Primacy of Institutions over Geography and Integration in Economic Development," *Journal of Economic Growth*, vol. 9, no. 2 (2004); and A. Aisen and Francisco José Veiga, "How Does Political Instability Affect Economic Growth," *European Journal of Political Economy*, vol. 29, no. 1 (2013).

In: African Growth and Opportunity Act
Editor: Hellen Edwards
ISBN: 978-1-63482-981-6

Chapter 3

AFRICAN GROWTH AND OPPORTUNITY ACT: LESSONS LEARNED FROM OTHER COUNTRIES' TRADE ARRANGEMENTS WITH SUB-SAHARAN AFRICA*

U.S. Government Accountability Office

February 25, 2015

Congressional Requesters

AFRICAN GROWTH AND OPPORTUNITY ACT: LESSONS LEARNED FROM OTHER COUNTRIES' TRADE ARRANGEMENTS WITH SUB-SAHARAN AFRICA

Trade preference programs were instituted by several advanced economies in the 1970s to help developing countries pursue economic development. The African Growth and Opportunity Act (AGOA), a U.S. trade preference program, was signed into law in 2000 and offers eligible sub-Saharan African (SSA) countries the ability to export qualifying goods to the United States

* This is an edited, reformatted and augmented version of a report, GAO-15-393R, issued February 25, 2015.

without import duties. Specifically, AGOA provides enhanced benefits to SSA countries under the auspices of the U.S. Generalized System of Preferences (GSP) program and provides duty-free, quota-free access for apparel items under specified conditions. The act supports efforts to reduce trade and investment barriers and negotiate reciprocal and mutually beneficial trade agreements between the United States and SSA countries. As of January 1, 2015, 39 SSA countries were eligible for AGOA benefits (AGOA countries).

The expiration of AGOA's authorization on September 30, 2015 provides Congress an opportunity to determine what, if any, changes may increase the program's effectiveness. Congressional requesters asked us to examine a range of issues relating to AGOA's effectiveness in promoting trade expansion and economic development, as well as factors affecting SSA trade with the United States and other countries. We addressed several of these issues, such as program eligibility reviews, in recent reports.[1] In this report, we examine how lessons learned from other countries' trade arrangements with SSA can clarify and provide insight into the trade-offs associated with making certain proposed modifications to AGOA. We briefed congressional requesters' staff on our preliminary findings on January 14, 2015. For the purposes of our briefing and this report, we focused on modifications the White House proposed in a 2014 strategy for investing in Africa trade.[2]

In conducting our work, we identified and reviewed documents and literature, including peer-reviewed academic articles, on AGOA and other countries' trade preference programs, trade agreements with AGOA countries, and SSA countries' participation in multilateral trade negotiations. In addition, we interviewed officials from the Departments of Agriculture, Commerce, State, and the Treasury; the Office of the U.S. Trade Representative (USTR); the U.S. International Trade Commission (USITC); and the U.S. Agency for International Development (USAID). We also conducted fieldwork in Geneva, Switzerland and Brussels, Belgium. We selected those locations for fieldwork based on our ability to interview multiple U.S. agency officials, African government officials,[3] government officials from countries with trade preference programs,[4] and representatives from think tanks and multilateral organizations with pertinent expertise. We did not independently assess the other countries' trade preference programs and agreements with SSA countries. The information on those programs and agreements is based on interviews and both primary (official) and other sources.[5] The lessons learned discussed herein are based on the views of those we interviewed as well as selected academic literature.

We conducted this performance audit from June 2014 to February 2015 in accordance with generally accepted government auditing standards. Those standards require that we plan and perform the audit to obtain sufficient, appropriate evidence to provide a reasonable basis for our findings and conclusions based on our audit objectives. We believe that the evidence obtained provides a reasonable basis for our findings and conclusions based on our audit objectives.

BACKGROUND

AGOA has been studied extensively, and many observers agree that it has been beneficial in helping expand trade between SSA countries and the United States. However, our prior work and available evidence suggest that AGOA has been only modestly effective in achieving its goals.[6]

Several distinct but interrelated program characteristics impact AGOA's scope, operation, and effectiveness, including the following:

- *Program duration*—the length of time during which the preferences are in effect.
- *Product coverage*—which products may receive tariff preferences. AGOA offers duty-free coverage of 97.5 percent of tariff lines for eligible least-developed countries (LDC) in sub-Saharan Africa according to analysis by the World Trade Organization (WTO) Secretariat. Most of the products excluded are agricultural products.
- *Rules of origin*—ensure that benefits of a preference program accrue to intended recipients by specifying a proportion of an imported product's value that must be produced in the preference beneficiary country. Rules of origin vary between different countries' preference programs and often from product to product within individual programs. For example, special rules are in effect that allow certain AGOA countries to export apparel tariff-free to the United States even if they use "Third Country" fabric— fabric from a country other than the United States or another AGOA country.
- *Program eligibility*—the ability of a country to qualify for participation in the program. Eligibility for AGOA includes meeting the statutory criteria to qualify for the program, as determined by

annual reviews of each SSA country that requests consideration for AGOA benefits.

One part of the White House's five-part strategy for investing in Africa trade, announced in August 2014, is to "Renew and Update AGOA to Increase Market Access Opportunities for Africa." It consists of the following four specific recommendations for AGOA modifications:[7]

- Approve a long-term extension of AGOA including "Third Country Fabric."
- Expand AGOA's product coverage.
- Improve rules of origin.
- Update eligibility criteria and review processes.

Three major developed countries have made significant modifications to their trade preference programs. Although their programs are more general in application than AGOA, which focuses on sub-Saharan Africa, the features of their programs provide insights into how AGOA might be affected or be made more effective by the White House's proposed modifications.

Other Countries' Programs Offer Insights into Trade-offs Associated with Proposed AGOA Modifications

In this section, for each of the President's four proposed modifications to AGOA, we (1) identify trade-offs associated with the proposed modification and (2) present insights derived from other developed countries' experiences.

Extending AGOA Reduces Risk to Investors, but Could Hinder U.S. Flexibility

Trade-offs

AGOA was initially authorized for 8 years; this authorization was subsequently extended through September 30, 2015 with enhanced benefits. The Third Country Fabric provision was authorized for a shorter period of time and has subsequently been extended several times.

President's Proposed Modification and Justification

Approve a Long Term Extension of AGOA including "Third Country Fabric"

A long-term extension of AGOA will offer greater certainty in the investment climate, help incentivize such investments and allow lesser-developed African beneficiaries to continue to develop the capacity to trade and take advantage of AGOA preferences.

Source: *The White House, Fact Sheet: Investing in African Trade for Our Common Future*, Aug. 4, 2014. | GAO-15-393R

The majority of the African government officials we interviewed supported the extension of AGOA for a longer period of time and thought that extending AGOA by 10 or 15 years could help support increased investment. An official we interviewed from one AGOA country said many jobs were eliminated in his country because companies moved their investments elsewhere to avoid the risk associated with delays in the renewal of AGOA's Third Country Fabric provision. Making that provision's authorization more predictable was also viewed as particularly important. According to officials from two AGOA countries, investors in the apparel sector need the assurance that AGOA benefits will cover their products for at least 9 months before they export them, because their production cycle includes planning for future seasons. Several studies note that the more flexible U.S. rule of origin introduced under the Third Country Fabric provision was largely responsible for significant increases in U.S. apparel imports under AGOA.

However, extending AGOA could reduce U.S. flexibility in making changes to its trading arrangement with SSA countries—including considering whether to pursue or insist upon free trade or reciprocal agreements. AGOA directed the President to develop a plan to negotiate and enter into Free Trade Agreements (FTA) with SSA partners, but negotiations have not yet been successful.[8] Regardless of the length of reauthorization, foreign trade experts believe that the United States would need to request another WTO waiver because participation in the program is limited to countries in a specific region (sub-Saharan Africa). According to U.S. and WTO officials, securing the requisite consent to the United States' request for the AGOA program's current WTO waiver proved to be a time-consuming and difficult task.[9]

Insights from Other Countries' Programs

The EU, Canada, and Japan reauthorized their programs for a decade, while making major changes to their programs. According to information from the European Commission, the EU, noting that importers and exporters needed stability and predictability to use preferences, changed the duration of its GSP scheme from 3 years to 10 years. However, trade experts noted that under EU market access regulations,[10] non-least developed countries (non-LDC) in the African, Caribbean, and Pacific region that had previously benefited from one-way preferences must have converted to reciprocal trade agreements known as Economic Partnership Agreements (EPA) by October 1, 2014, or revert to the EU's less generous GSP program if they were still eligible.[11] The EU initialed its first three EPAs with regional groups of SSA countries in July 2014 and October 2014.[12] According to trade experts, the EPAs provide EU exporters favorable access in their markets, relative to others such as the United States. According to information from the European Commission and Canadian government, the EU and Canada also lowered the cut-off point for graduating countries, as explained more fully below. According to information from the WTO Secretariat and the Japanese Ministry of Foreign Affairs, Japan instituted a partial graduation mechanism and graduated numerous products from China. Sources indicate that the revised programs incorporate ongoing review of country and product eligibility in line with established, internationally developed criteria. Thus, while the overall programs are stable, country and product participation is subject to change and will continue to evolve.

Increasing Product Coverage Could Increase Exports, but May Raise Concerns among U.S. Domestic Producers

President's Proposed Modification and Justification

Expand AGOA's Product Coverage

AGOA already provides duty-free access for 97.5 percent of all tariff lines for virtually all AGOA beneficiaries. However, there are 316 tariff lines – most covering agricultural products – that are not currently included. While these products have historically been import sensitive, it is important to examine whether any products can now be added to AGOA.

Source: *The White House, Fact Sheet: Investing in African Trade for Our Common Future*, Aug. 4, 2014. | GAO-15-393R

Trade-offs

Foreign officials note that adding some currently excluded products to AGOA, particularly those in the agricultural sector, could provide greater benefits to Africa. Many African countries' exports are highly concentrated in a few products, and some of Africa's most important and globally competitive export products are still excluded from available preference programs. For example, the 2013 Africa Competitiveness Report recently noted that countries such as Burundi, Côte d'Ivoire, Ethiopia, and Malawi are highly dependent on agricultural exports.[13] The USITC has noted that although AGOA countries produce a wide range of products with export potential to the United States—mostly agricultural products, handicrafts and woodcrafts, and leather and leather products—some are currently ineligible for AGOA preferences. Further, trade experts noted that products such as sugar, meat, dairy, and peanuts face volume limitations and higher U.S. tariffs on "over quota" amounts of exports subject to tariff-rate quotas EU.

However, certain domestic commodity groups have raised concerns over possible increases in imports, and statutory constraints on adding products to AGOA's coverage exist. U.S. government officials we met with said that U.S. producers have expressed concern that removing tariffs on products would result in increased imports that might adversely affect those industries. Further, certain statutory and policy constraints have been placed on the President in designating products as eligible for tariff-free treatment. For example, the GSP statute, which provides authority for much of AGOA's enhanced coverage under GSP, precludes the President from designating certain articles as eligible for GSP duty-free treatment. [15] The President also must seek USITC advice on import sensitivity when making determinations on product coverage. Also by statute, agricultural products subject to tariff-rate quotas may only enjoy duty-free access up to the "in quota" amount. One U.S. trade expert recently noted that the United States has made commitments to certain trading partners in trade agreements on some agricultural products subject to TRQs, such as Australia (beef), and Argentina (peanuts).[16]

Insights from the EU's Program

EU officials in Brussels told us that EU agriculture industry representatives had expressed concerns when the EU was contemplating expansion of preferences to cover previously excluded agriculture products under the Everything but Arms (EBA) program that removing tariffs on products would result in increased imports that might adversely affect their industries. However, they said that the feared increase in imports did not materialize, largely because of lack of capacity within Africa to produce or export the quantity of products that would have negatively impacted EU industries. (Some recent empirical studies also suggest that expanded preferential access would not negatively impact U.S. agricultural interests on similar grounds.)[17] According to trade experts, for two of the most import-sensitive products, sugar and rice, the EU phased in duty-free access under EBA and made complementary modifications to its Common Agricultural Policy to mitigate any adverse impacts.[18]

Easing Rules of Origin Could Address African Concerns and Increase Use of AGOA Preferences, but May Also Benefit Non-AGOA Countries

President's Proposed Modification and Justification

Improve Rules of Origin

AGOA offers some of the most flexible rules of origin of any U.S. trade arrangement. In an effort to update the rules, however, the Administration is working to identify ways to provide greater flexibility, encourage regional integration and the development of regional value chains, and incentivize more U.S.-Africa trade.

Source: The White House, Fact Sheet: Investing in African Trade for Our Common Future, Aug. 4, 2014. | GAO-15-393R

Trade-offs

Revising AGOA rules of origin to be more flexible could address several concerns. Although rules of origin are an integral component of any preference program, officials we met with told us that they consider AGOA rules of origin to be complex and difficult to understand. Two foreign trade experts said that AGOA rules of origin add an administrative burden because of the associated strict recordkeeping requirements. Others suggested that AGOA (and GSP) rules of origin are outdated and have not (materially) changed since they were developed in the 1970s. Since then, the nature of manufacturing production has changed, becoming a more globally networked process with inputs competitively sourced among numerous suppliers. Rules of origin that are not flexible enough to account for this change may adversely affect SSA competitiveness and result in some of the available preferences not being utilized. Some foreign trade experts have noted that allowing beneficiaries to count inputs from other countries toward meeting rules of origin requirements (known as cumulation) may address some of these problems and encourage integration into existing supplier networks.

If AGOA rules of origin become more flexible, however, the likelihood increases that non-AGOA countries will profit from AGOA benefits. Devising ways to avoid this possible outcome is important to ensure that only beneficiary countries receive preferences under the AGOA program. Cumulation has been widely recognized as helpful in principle, and presently, AGOA permits some cumulation among SSA beneficiaries. However, AGOA generally does not expressly permit cumulation with other GSP recipients or with FTA partners.[19]

Insights from Other Countries' Programs

Canada and the EU have updated and revised their rules of origin in an effort to make them easier for developing countries to understand and to meet, according to a WTO document. Notably, it indicated that Canada and the EU have

- widened the scope for cumulation of inputs from multiple countries to attain the required value-added threshold,[20] and
- relaxed certain product-specific rules for LDC beneficiaries.

Foreign trade experts and officials we met cited Canada's broadened scope for cumulation as helpful in increasing preference utilization. Views on the EU's change were more mixed, in part, they noted, because the EU still has a host of product-specific rules, and in part because the EU will only allow cumulation between GSP beneficiaries and FTA partners upon specific request by the beneficiary, with EU approval subject to several conditions. Preliminary evidence based on trade data indicates that Canada's and the EU's eased rules of origin for textiles and apparel have increased program utilization. The changes to product-specific rules that Canada and the EU made, however, would appear to give their programs features similar to AGOA's Third Country Fabric provision, which allows most AGOA beneficiaries to use fabric from a country other than the United States or another AGOA country.

Revising Eligibility Criteria Could Limit Preferences to Fewer Countries, but May Negatively Impact Regional Integration

President's Proposed Modification and Justification

Update Eligibility Criteria and Review Processes

AGOA's eligibility criteria and review processes have not been updated since its launch, notwithstanding changes in African and global trade practices over the last 14 years. The Administration is working to identify ways that the criteria can be updated to address current challenges and to improve effectiveness of the review processes.

Source: The White House, Fact Sheet: Investing in African Trade for Our Common Future, Aug. 4, 2014. | GAO-15-393R

Trade-offs

Updating AGOA eligibility criteria could allow the United States to address the challenge of ensuring that preferences are focused on helping those countries that have the greatest need to increase and diversify their exports. AGOA authorizes the President each year to designate an SSA country as eligible for AGOA trade preferences if the President determines that the country has met or is making continual progress toward meeting AGOA's eligibility criteria, among other requirements.[21] In addition, the act requires that an SSA country be eligible for GSP in order to be considered for AGOA benefits. One of the determinants of eligibility is the country's income level. Countries are not eligible for AGOA (or the U.S. GSP) if they are classified by the World Bank as high-income countries.[22] Countries that exceed that threshold graduate out.

One concern in changing eligibility criteria such as by lowering the income threshold for graduation, as the EU and Canada have done, is that it may result in graduation of major African economies and thus have the adverse impact of disrupting trade for neighboring countries, which could in turn potentially undermine regional integration. [23] For example, according to a WTO official, if South Africa became ineligible for AGOA benefits, its AGOAeligible neighbors might no longer be able to qualify their exports for AGOA treatment because product inputs imported from South Africa would no longer count toward the percentage of the final product that must be "domestic" in order to export tariff-free under AGOA. African government officials we met with also said that other countries in the region suffered when Madagascar was suspended from AGOA.

Insights from Other Countries' Programs

Both the EU and Canada now systematically graduate countries from their trade preference programs. Specifically, the EU recently revised its eligibility criteria to drop countries as trade preference beneficiaries if they (1) qualify for the World Bank's Upper-Middle-Income category or (2) can access the EU market through another preferential regime. In Canada, countries lose preference benefits if they either qualify for the World Bank's Upper-Middle-Income category or have exports that account for at least 1 percent of world exports for 2 consecutive years. As a result, numerous beneficiaries graduated from their preference programs for developing countries—72 in Canada and 87 in the EU.[24] African nations affected by these changes include South Africa, Kenya, and Mauritius. The EU cited a movement in the last decade toward greater differentiation among beneficiary countries in terms of development, trade, and financial needs, and noted that more advanced developing countries are now competitive on a global scale. It further noted that prior to the modification, 40 percent of the EU's preferential imports were accounted for by the more advanced countries.

However, Canada and the EU took several preemptive steps to mitigate any disruptions caused by this change, according to information from the Canadian government and the European Commission. For example, Canada

- grandfathered inputs from prior beneficiaries for LDCs;
- will permit duty-free entry of apparel from graduated countries if they incorporate Canadian textiles; and
- made sugar duty-free on a global basis to prevent disruption of supplies that had been duty-free under GSP for Brazil, which Canada graduated.

Concluding Observations

Each of the President's proposed modifications to AGOA—enacting a long-term program extension, increasing product coverage, making rules of origin more flexible, and updating eligibility criteria and review processes—involve complex trade-offs. In reviewing other countries' modifications to their preference programs, we noted that they recognized that making changes in one area could impact performance in other areas, and therefore took proactive steps to counter or complement them. For example, the EU's and Canada's decade-long extension of their programs did not lock them into offering preferences to countries for the entire decade because they also tightened their eligibility criteria. In addition, Canada's revised rules of origin allow LDCs to use inputs from graduated countries and still qualify for preferences in recognition that graduating countries such as South Africa could disrupt regionally integrated supply chains in neighboring countries such as Lesotho or Botswana. Analyzing ways in which these program characteristics were recalibrated may prove useful in weighing which changes to AGOA are most likely to increase SSA exports and help SSA countries integrate into the global economy.

AGENCY COMMENTS

We are not making recommendations in this report. We provided a draft of this report to USTR and USDA for comment. They provided technical comments, which we incorporated as appropriate.

Kimberly Gianopoulos
Director, International Affairs and Trade

End Notes

[1] GAO, African Growth and Opportunity Act: Eligibility Process and Economic Development in Sub-Saharan Africa, GAO-15-300 (Washington, D.C.: Feb. 12, 2015); African Growth and Opportunity Act: USAID Could Enhance Utilization by Working with More Countries to Develop Export Strategies, GAO-15-218 (Washington, D.C.: Jan. 22, 2015); and African Growth and Opportunity Act: Observations on Competitiveness and Diversification of U.S. Imports from Beneficiary Countries, GAO-14-722R (Washington, D.C.: July 21, 2014).

[2] The White House, Fact Sheet: Investing in African Trade for Our Common Future (Washington, D.C.: Aug. 4, 2014), accessed February 12, 2015, http://www.whitehouse.gov/the-press-office/2014/08/04/fact-sheet-investing-africantrade-our-common-future.

[3] We interviewed African government officials from Ethiopia, Lesotho, Mauritius, Nigeria, South Africa, and Uganda— countries we selected because they represent a range of sizes, face a range of trade challenges, and actively use AGOA benefits.

[4] We interviewed government officials from Australia, Brazil, Canada, China, and the European Union (EU)—countries we selected based on the amount of trade they conducted with SSA countries, congressional interest in their trade programs, and whether they had made recent modifications to their trade programs that related to the White House's proposed modifications to AGOA. We refer to the EU as a country for the purpose of this report.

[5] Information on Japan's program and changes is based on official information that Japan provided to the World Trade Organization (WTO) Secretariat, which made it publicly available through the WTO's preferential trade arrangement portal. WTO, Preferential Trade Arrangements Database, accessed February 18, 2015, http://ptadb.wto.org/?lang=1.

[6] GAO, U.S.-Africa Trade: Options for Congressional Consideration to Improve Textile and Apparel Sector Competitiveness under the African Growth and Opportunity Act, GAO-09-916 (Washington, D.C.: Aug. 12, 2009); GAO, International Trade: U.S. Trade Preference Programs Provide Important Benefits, but a More Integrated Approach Would Better Ensure Programs Meet Shared Goals, GAO-08-443 (Washington, D.C.: Mar. 7, 2008); and USITC, AGOA: Trade and Investment Performance Overview, Publication No. 4461, April 2014.

[7] The other four parts of the strategy are: Find Synergies through Aligning Assistance; Improve Infrastructure to Enhance Competitiveness; Strengthen Trade Capacity Building, Value Added Production, and Supply Chains to Increase AGOA Utilization; and Create New Markets for Africa.

[8] Francisco Sanchez, Undersecretary of International Trade, U.S. Department of Commerce, responses to questions submitted for the record by Senator James M. Inhofe. S. HRG. 112–653 (2012) 60-61. Sanchez indicated that the East African Community was not ready or willing to conclude a high standard FTA with the United States and that a U.S. effort to conclude an FTA with the Southern African Customs Union was also abandoned.

[9] The AGOA program's current WTO waiver and the AGOA program's authorization both expire on September 30, 2015.

[10] EU Market Access Regulation MAR 1528/2007, Dec. 20, 2007; EU Market Access Regulation MAR 527/2013, May 21, 2013.

[11] According to foreign government and trade officials we spoke with in Geneva and Brussels, the EU's decision to shift to reciprocal agreements was driven in part by the EU's loss of two WTO disputes involving preferences as well as the 2007 expiration of its WTO waiver pertaining to EU preferences for African, Caribbean, and Pacific countries.

[12] The EU has signed EPAs with the East African Community; the Southern African Development Community, which includes the Southern African Customs Union and South Africa; and the Economic Community of West African States, which includes its 15 members plus Mauritania.

[13] The World Economic Forum, the World Bank, the African Development Bank, and the Ministry of Foreign Affairs of Denmark, The Africa Competitiveness Report 2013 (Geneva: 2013), 41.

[14] A tariff-rate quota includes a lower, "in quota" tariff that applies to a limited quantity of imports, and a higher, often prohibitive, "over quota" tariff that applies to any imports that exceed the quota. The quantity in the "in quota" level must be made available in accordance with specific allocation rules and other international commitments.

[15] See 19 USC 2463.

[16] Kimberly Ann Elliott, AGOA's Final Frontier: Removing US Farm Trade Barriers (Center for Global Development: July 28, 2014), accessed February 18, 2015, http://www.cgdev.org/publication/ft/agoa-final-frontier-removing-us-farmtrade-barriers.

[17] Antoine Bouët, David Laborde Debucquet, Elisa Dienesch, and Kimberly Elliott, "The Costs and Benefits of Duty-Free, Quota-Free Access for Poor Countries: Who and What Matters?," International Food Policy Research Institute Discussion Paper 00990 (June 2010); Simon Mevel, Zenia Lewis, Mwangi S. Kimenyi, Stephen Karingi, and Anne Kamau, "The African Growth and Opportunity Act: An Empirical Analysis of the Possibilities Post-2015," Africa Growth Initiative at Brookings (Brookings Institution: July 2013). Others note limitations to the general equilibrium models used in these studies and that greater market access in agriculture could keep LDCs from diversifying their exports into more dynamic sectors of the economy. See Massimiliano Cali and Sheila Page, "Reforming Trade Preferences for LDCs," Opinion 145, Overseas Development Institute (June 2010).

[18] Alan Matthews and Jacques Gallezot, "The role of EBA in the political economy of CAP reform," in Institute for International Integration Studies Discussion Paper Series, No. 133 (Dublin: Trinity College Dublin, April 2006), accessed February 22, 2015, https://www.tcd.ie/iiis/documents/ discussion/pdfs/iiisdp133.pdf.

[19] Cumulation under GSP is limited to specified regional groups. Within sub-Saharan Africa, two regional groups are specified: members of the West African Economic and Monetary Union and SADC are potentially eligible for the cumulation benefit.

[20] In Canada's case, cumulation is allowed across GSP and GSP-LDC preference beneficiaries and, in the case of the EU, between GSP and FTA/EPA partners, as noted in a WTO document.

[21] See Pub. L. No. 106-200, May 18, 2000, section 104(a)(1). For a discussion of how this process operates and how U.S. officials use it to engage with SSA countries on their progress towards economic, political, and development reform objectives, see GAO-15-300.

[22] Countries that reach high-income status are ineligible, but 60 days' advance notice must be provided to Congress and the pertinent recipient, and a transition period of one to two years is provided to the recipient.

[23] Equatorial Guinea was the first and only country to be excluded from potential eligibility for AGOA because it exceeded the current high-income threshold. Of the current AGOA beneficiaries, Angola, Gabon, Mauritius, Namibia, Seychelles, and South Africa were Upper-Middle-Income countries in the World Bank's Country Income Classification table. See the World Bank, Country and Lending Groups, accessed February 18, 2015, http://data.worldbank.org/about/country-and-lending-groups.

[24] According to information from the Canadian government and the European Commission, the beneficiary changes were effective January 1, 2014 for the EU and January 1, 2015 for Canada.

r U.S. government entities.

[2] D. Acemoglu, S. Johnson, and J.A. Robinson, "The Colonial Origins of Comparative Development: An Empirical Investigation," *American Economic Review*, vol. 91, no.5 (2001); D. Rodrik, A. Subramanian, and F. Trebbi, "Institutions Rule: The Primacy of Institutions over Geography and Integration in Economic Development," *Journal of Economic Growth*, vol. 9, no. 2 (2004); and A. Aisen and Francisco José Veiga, "How Does Political Instability Affect Economic Growth," *European Journal of Political Economy*, vol. 29, no. 1 (2013).

INDEX

D

E

F

G

H

I

J

K

L

M

N

O

P

T

U

V

W

Z